T0348992

ALSO BY JUDITH VIORST

Making the Best of What's Left

WHEN WE'RE TOO OLD TO GET
THE CHAIRS REUPHOLSTERED

Judith Viorst

Simon & Schuster

NEW YORK   AMSTERDAM/ANTWERP   LONDON
TORONTO   SYDNEY/MELBOURNE   NEW DELHI

Simon & Schuster
1230 Avenue of the Americas
New York, NY 10020

First Simon & Schuster hardcover edition April 2025

SIMON & SCHUSTER and colophon are registered trademarks of Simon & Schuster, LLC

Simon & Schuster strongly believes in freedom of expression and stands against censorship in all its forms. For more information, visit BooksBelong.com.

For information about special discounts for bulk purchases, please contact Simon & Schuster Special Sales at 1-866-506-1949 or business@simonandschuster.com.

The Simon & Schuster Speakers Bureau can bring authors to your live event. For more information or to book an event, contact the Simon & Schuster Speakers Bureau at 1-866-248-3049 or visit our website at www.simonspeakers.com.

Book text design by Paul Dippolito

Manufactured in the United States of America

10 9 8 7 6 5 4 3 2 1

Library of Congress Cataloging-in-Publication Data is available.

ISBN 978-1-6680-6801-4
ISBN 978-1-6680-6803-8 (ebook)

For Milton

One Last Time

In the meantime . . . enjoy not being dead.

—Joan Retallack

Contents

Making the Best of What's Left

About This Book

Milton, my husband of almost sixty-three years, died in December 2022. He wasn't supposed to die before me—I told him this was something he COULD NOT DO—but when did he listen? I write, in this book, about widowhood, but I also want to explore the challenges that I and the people I've talked with—comfortably middle-class family people like me—have been dealing with in these years beyond age eighty, in what I'm calling the Final Fifth of life.

Changes in our body and brain. Changes in where we're living. Changes in what we can and no longer can do. Figuring out how to balance freedom and loneliness. And maybe mulling over a question or two, like: Do I or don't I believe in some kind of Afterlife? And would I be open to finding another mate? And must I quickly dispose of my dead husband's clothes—or can I wait until I'm really ready? And how long do I get to say I'm not really ready?

And then there's the question of whether it would or wouldn't be woefully wasteful—with time running out! at the age of ninety-four!—to have a couple of fraying chairs reupholstered.

*

I wish I could discuss this, as I did so many things, with my had-an-opinion-on-practically-everything husband. Even though there were times when marriage to someone with an opinion on practically everything could drive the person married to him berserk.

In a poem that I'd planned to give him, but didn't get the chance to give him, on Valentine's Day, I tried to convey the realities of our long marriage. It's called "A Valentine for the Extremely Married," and it wasn't meant to be tested anytime soon.

A Valentine for the Extremely Married

Today is Valentine's Day

And once again I want to say

I'm crazy about you.

And though I sometimes wish

That you were dead,

This doesn't mean

That I could live

Without you.

But now I'm living without him, in a place I'm only beginning to learn to call home.

Home

Soon after we moved away I awoke in the middle of the night, sat up in bed, and announced, "I want to go home.

"I want to go home," I repeated, insistently.

And then, as I slowly sank back into sleep, I said it one more time: "I want to go home!"

Like Dorothy in the Land of Oz, like Ronald Colman shut out of Shangri-La, I wasn't where I belonged, where I needed to be. How did I get here? Why did I come here? What the hell was I thinking? And—most important—when could I go home?

As best I can recall I never loved any physical object the way I loved our rambling old house in the Cleveland Park section of Washington, D.C. The moment that I first saw it, peering in from its sumptuous wraparound front porch, I said to my husband, loudly, "I can't live without it." Milton tried to shush me, on the grounds that my over-the-top enthusiasm would prompt the real estate agent to raise the asking price, but all I could do was keep saying, "I can't live without it."

And for fifty-one years I didn't have to.

*

At the time of this mid-night awakening my husband and I had been living for eight or nine weeks in this pleasant in-town retirement community (RC), having left our seven-bedrooms, five-fireplaces Victorian house for a space that felt like a cabin on a cruise ship. Surrounded by the drastically downsized furnishings and tchotchkes of decades and decades and decades of acquisition, we were certainly in the company of familiars. But they weren't in our house, a house we'd adored every single day that we had lived there, a house that belonged to us and that we belonged to. Hadn't I, wrapping my arms around one of the stately Ionic columns of our front porch, proclaimed on many occasions, "I plan to die here"? Or had I already died and, along with Milton, been assigned to this genial, two-bedrooms-and-a-den Afterlife?

Well, I guess I knew the answer to how I got here—to how *we* got here. We got here thanks to the exigencies of old age. Milton, a serious lifelong jock, who swam a hundred laps in the pool every day, and who gracefully skied expert trails well into his eighties, now suffered from badly compromised vision, a heart condition, vertigo, an arthritic foot that made it hard to walk, and assorted other diminishments that had prompted his team of specialists to unitedly urge him to give up a house with stairs. Meanwhile, I, who had fallen and broken my pelvis that past May, was basically out of commission for a few months, forcing our adult children to deal with two impaired parents at once, a situation that—all of us quickly recognized—was probably only the first in a forthcoming series of multiple medical misfortunes.

Vanity prompts me to add, before continuing with this account, that I didn't actually *fall* down—I was pushed. Not out of malice or carelessness but because, as I walked ahead of him on the way to consult a doctor about his balance problems, Milton lost his balance, tottered, fell forward, and crash-banged into me, knocking me to the sidewalk and then landing full force on top of my prostrate body. He got a few little scratches on his nose; I got a bunch of broken bones in my pelvis.

Wheeled on his-and-her stretchers into the hospital ER we were greeted by a young doctor who, thrilled to hear that we were husband and wife, clasped his hands and crowed, "My first married couple!" I wasn't that thrilled to make his list of firsts.

Milton went home that day while I was stuck with a longer stay—a week of healing, then two of inpatient therapy. Our sons, Tony and Nick and Alexander, along with a variety of home health aides, cared for Milton while I was gone, with friends signed up to deliver a multitude of magnificent meals and keep him company. Everything went well, I was told, until I returned and started taking over, shortly after which the screaming began.

It went something like this:

Milton with cane, wobbling his way up the stairs. A harried home health aide, racing to get behind him. Me on my walker, shrieking impotently.

YOU CANNOT GO UP OR DOWN THE STAIRS ALONE. YOU ARE GOING TO FALL AND HIT YOUR HEAD AND GET BRAIN DAMAGE. YOU AREN'T STEADY ON YOUR FEET. YOU'RE GOING TO FALL AND GET BRAIN DAMAGE. YOU'RE GOING TO WIND UP COMPLETELY RUINING OUR LIVES.

Though I never reproached him, or even brought it up, I've always suspected that Milton thought I was trying to make him feel guilty for losing his balance and breaking the bones in my pelvis. Which I wasn't. I truly wasn't. I swear I wasn't. Not because I am far too noble for such lowdown maneuvers, but simply because my husband does not do guilt. It's not in his nature. It's not in his DNA. It's not the result of some trauma in early childhood. But sixty-plus years of marriage have made it maddeningly clear that there's no point in trying to lay a guilt trip on Milton. It will not succeed. My husband doesn't do guilt.

Nor is he much better at doing compliance.

Milton, I explain to all of the frustrated hardworking health aides who were finding him, shall we say, challenging to manage, is a basically very decent, very kindhearted, well-meaning

man who is very very used to being very very very independent. Which is why, I further explain, they really should not
take it personally if he says, "Get your [expletives deleted]
hands off of me" when they monitor his trips up and down the
stairs. Or to and from other perilous places. As for the aide who
wept while she told me, "I love him like my father. I love him
but he makes it hard to help him," I assured her that, in spite of
some extremely unfatherly moments, he loved her too.

In addition to talking to Milton's aides, I also talked to
myself—about screaming less and accepting the inevitable, the
inevitable being the fact that one of these days he would ruin
our lives by falling down the stairs and getting brain damage.

Unless . . . Unless . . . Unless we moved to a place where you
didn't need stairs. A place where you could get around without
stairs. A place that not only required no stairs but perhaps offered other perks that could compensate two early-ninety-year-
olds for giving up their treasured, beloved house.

Like the drip-drip-drip of a water faucet that cannot be shut
off, the move-move-move message, once started, never let up,
amplified by our children who, though they too adored our
house, thought that it was time for us to go. Whenever I've
talked to friends who have moved from family homes to retirement communities, I've found that while some have been
pressed or persuaded to do so by their children, most had their
own good reasons to make that choice. To make it before it

was forced upon them by circumstances. To make it while that choice was still theirs to make. To make it because they'd be physically safer, have fewer burdensome household responsibilities, be part of a caring cohort, be offered a right-there range of mind and body activities, and be hopefully less dependent on devoted but otherwise occupied sons and daughters, especially those three thousand miles away.

It was time to make this monumental change. And it was, indeed, a monumental change, involving for Milton and me several difficult stages: the stage of why should we leave, which was followed by how could we bear to leave, which was followed by when could we possibly leave, which was followed by where will we go if we leave. And as we worked our way through these various stages of leaving and losing and letting go, our D.C. son, Alexander, and his super-awesome wife, Marla, with some serious help from our equally awesome friend Li, were (initially unbeknownst to us) busily checking out apartment options. Until they found one, flooded with sunshine and set among the trees of Rock Creek Park, a small but charming apartment in a retirement community, which was just a short drive from our old house and where half a dozen friends lived, and more were heading.

I especially liked the fact that we'd be living right here in the city and not out of town—not in one of those places that felt a lot like another galaxy or an ice floe on which the old folks were sent out to sea. I also liked that I already knew the streets, shops, and restaurants of this neighborhood, for I suffer from what I've chosen to call "geographical dyslexia," which means, as my friend Nell once put it, that I could get lost in a restaurant with a salad bar. Being fully familiar with this part of Northwest D.C. would save me many months of helplessly driving around and around—in circles, in confusion, and in tears.

So finding a place to live turned out to be easier than we'd expected. As did finding the buyers for our house, the ache of losing it somewhat soothed by selling to two lovely women and their three daughters, each the age of our own young sons when we moved there. On the other hand, divesting ourselves of fifteen thousand books, plus rooms and rooms and still more rooms of furnishings, and outdoor chairs and tables and chaises and sculpture, and a kitchen equipped with enough sets of pots and pans and dishes and silver to entertain legions, was— despite the help of our indispensable packers and movers and a supremely able assistant named Ruth Anne—breathtakingly painful. In addition I had to face the fact, as I gasped at all the stuff we'd stashed and forgotten, that Milton and I had, willy-nilly, become the Collyer brothers, those notorious hoarders who never let go of anything.

Considering that we were moving to an apartment designed for one fairly skinny person, we needed to give away, throw away, sell, or store in storage units much of what we'd been living with most of our lives. And so we did. And oh, how much I miss them.

I miss my embroidered yellow velvet chair. I miss my authentic Early American hutch table. I miss the abandoned leaves of my dining room table, which, when opened, seated twelve. And I miss my battered but beautiful antique piano, which would never stay in tune and which our piano tuner liked to call a "whore," meaning, he explained, that "it was gorgeous on the outside, and absolutely rotten on the inside." I probably should have lectured him on the dignity of sex work, but all I only said was, "I love my piano."

And now it's gone, along with everything else that won't fit into our small apartment. Which Marla enthusiastically calls our tree house and which some of our friends are uneasily calling "cozy." Which provides not a kitchen but a kitchenette. And which offers, instead of an icemaker, one measly ice tray. Seduced by the sunlit rooms and the fluttering greenery that filled every single window and turned the beige walls a pale green in the late afternoon, Milton and I decided to make our move.

Once upon a time—though it hasn't worked out that way—we assumed Alexander and Marla and their three children would be the next family to occupy our house. Our model was the family next door—three generations of Carters and of Grogans, an arrangement that ended when the seven Grogan sons and daughters sold the house. Before they left, however, they did something that I found enormously touching. They organized a ritual farewell, with a priest presiding—his readings included Rumi, an Aztec prayer, and Milne's Pooh Bear—and family members exchanging funny, fond, sometimes painful memories of the rich and zesty life that they had shared. I loved the respect and attention they had chosen to pay to their history in that house. So I arranged to do the same for ours.

Which was why, one November weekend, with most of our family gathered to say a final farewell, I was telling them about falling in love with this house, and remembering some of the things I loved best about it, and repeating some of our often-told family stories, and asking each one of them—the sons, the daughters-in-law, the grandkids—to talk about what this house had meant to them.

It was, we all agreed, a truly user-friendly house, with almost nothing too fragile to be endangered, making it easy to welcome the bumptious kiddies and hairy teens who were always eating and sleeping over on weekends. And since my role as hostess involved just throwing some extra spaghetti into the pot or some blankets over the bodies asleep on the floor, and since Milton and I (with some very few exceptions) really liked the kids our kids hung out with, we were happy our house was a hangout, happy to have created, as our oldest son, Tony, put it, "a powerful, powerful gravitational pull."

But we weren't always softies, as all three of our sons pointed out, recalling their father's rule that any kid who planned to sleep over on Friday night was expected to work on our house and our yard on Saturday. To do some scraping, some painting, some weeding, some hammering of loose shingles. To do what every kid remembered was called (in French) the corvée, originally defined as unpaid work required of a vassal by his lord. Peculiar as this still seems, the corvée was and remains among the fondest of our family memories.

Our house also held sweet memories of visits from Ben and Nathaniel, our New York grandkids, and from Miranda and Bryce, our Denver grandkids, but especially from our D.C. grandkids—Olivia, Isaac, and Toby—whose weekly Saturday visits, in their years somewhere between toddlerhood and teens, swept us into a whirlwind of activity. Fueled by bowls of Milton's famous pasta or grilled-cheese sandwiches, we started with stoopball on the front steps of our house, the kids indicating their disapproval of my sluggish pace with frequent cries of "Juju, move your booty!" We then went around to the playground with Milton to play some two-on-three basketball, (accompanied by more "move your booty" cries), then back to the house for some indoor hide-and-seek, with Milton—instead of hiding—seeking a nap. And after I'd tracked down Toby on a shelf in the linen closet and Olivia covered with pillows behind a chair, and Isaac (wearing my shower cap) crouched in our shower, the kids and I, using three full decks of cards, carpeted all of the living room floor with an intricate, truly magnificent two-story card house. The visit usually ended with me and the children on the couch, reading Shel Silverstein's wilder poems aloud. Then Alexander would pick up the kids and I'd give serious thought to maybe starting the cocktail hour early.

Although it was still rather early in the day, I sometimes felt it was time for some Chardonnay.

And there always was time in our house for celebrations: Grammar school, high school, and college graduations. Passovers and Thanksgivings with the Pitofskys, whose friendships with us have spanned three generations. Engagement parties, marriage parties, political parties, book-publication parties. Ten- and fifty- and ninety-year-old birthday parties.

And now a party to honor and say goodbye to and tell some stories about this house.

And of course I could not resist telling the story I've told a thousand times before, which happened a few days after we had moved in:

I was admiring my home office—I'd never actually ever had my own office before—when the telephone rang. A veddy veddy aristocratic voice announced it was Libby Rowe on the line. She quickly came to the point: "I certainly do not wish to be a nosy neighbor, but do you actually WANT your three little boys to be sitting outside on the roof of your house?" I screamed. I dropped the phone. I ran upstairs. And there, exploring the boundaries of their new residence, were three Viorst boys sitting—yes!—on the roof.

In our house there was plenty of talking and plenty of laughing and plenty of yelling, and it wasn't only the boys who were making the noise. Indeed, I reminisced, I sometimes ran around the house shutting the windows so our neighbors wouldn't hear Milton and me going at it. And Nick remembered being assured that, in spite of these top-volume carryings-on, we would never ever divorce, that the screaming and yelling we did were INSTEAD of divorce.

Alexander's contribution to our household history began: "There were two times I almost burned down the house." By the time he finished describing how, at age twelve, he decided to test his new kerosene camping stove by lighting it in the middle of his bedroom, I was too shaken up to attend to the second story, about the next time that he almost burned down the house.

At the end of our formal farewell we had invited the other families who lived on our block to join us for mini-cupcakes and Prosecco. A few days later, we watched the moving trucks arriving at our front door, and I started the process of redefining "home."

As sensible. As safe. As our sensible safe retirement community.

Our Sensible Safe Retirement Community

There's yoga and book clubs and lectures to keep ourselves perking.

No stairs to be climbed and no dinners we have to prepare.

It isn't our problem to solve when the furnace stops working.

It isn't our problem to solve when the roof needs repair.

There are buttons a person can press in an emergency,

A beauty salon specializing in grey thinning hair,

Bathrooms galore for that can't-wait-a-minute-more urgency.

And whenever we need to sit down there's always a chair.

In our sensible safe retirement community

There's pickleball, poker games, concerts, a pool, Sunday prayer,

And other amenities promising us immunity

From all of those late-in-life challenges lurking Out There.

Yes, everything's wonderful, marvelous, swell—good as
gold.

Except for this one little problem:

Everyone's old.

Old

We can stroll on our RC's pretty paths but we aren't likely to see some six-year-old proudly navigating his bicycle. Nor are there young lovers, or pregnant women, or teenagers tethered to their earbuds populating its tasteful public rooms. And when we dress up for some special event like Oktober Fest, Arabian Nights, Christmas Eve, the dominant fashions will still have elasticized waistbands, the universal accessory will still be either the walker or the cane, and the only genuine color of hair (I still dye mine brown, but who do I think I'm kidding?) remains, by a landside, fifty shades of grey.

Everyone looks put-together. And some look very attractive indeed. But we all look like advertisements for memory supplements.

Old isn't just a state of mind, no matter how perky and positive we may be. It's also a nonnegotiable reality. Our body no longer does all the things we want it to do. Our choices are far more constricted, far less free. We once, in our family, our work, our duties and pleasures, had some meaningful standing, some true authority. But at eighty, at eighty-five, at over ninety, we find ourselves emeritus, definitively demoted, diminished in status, influence, and control.

For it's been a good number of years since our retirement party. Our grandchildren, not just our children, are pretty well grown. And though we in Independent Living are, for the most part, living on our own, we're increasingly being regarded by our family and younger friends, and by strangers we encounter, and even by people we're talking to on the phone, as old folks who could use a little help.

So they helpfully put our suitcase up in the baggage compartment. Hand on our elbow, they guide us across the street. If we're taking the bus or the subway they will often jump up and offer us their seat. And after whoever we're talking to at the other end of the line finds out how old we are, they immediately start speaking slower and louder, and calling us names like "hon" or "sweetie" or "dear."

And of course we're feeling grateful to them. Of course we are! But some of us may be feeling annoyed as well. For they're treating us as if we're a Little Old Man or a Little Old Lady. And maybe we secretly thought they couldn't tell.

They can usually tell.

In a recent reminder I wasn't a girl of seventy-two anymore, I went to the supermarket to do some shopping. But when I was finished and trying to exit the parking garage, my ticket—though properly stamped and properly dated—failed to make the garage gate open up. No matter which way I slid the ticket into the ticket machine, the gate repeatedly refused to open. Eventually the driver behind me, having waited patiently for a while, stopped being patient and started honking his horn. And though he kept on honking, and I kept frantically trying to get my ticket to work, and more and more cars kept lining up behind us, the (expletives deleted) gate wouldn't open.

And then I saw a man—salvation!—pushing his cart to his car, and I pleadingly called him over: "Sir, can you help me?" And after I'd finished explaining (while the car behind me kept honking) the fix I was in, he looked at my ticket, looked at the gate, and then he said to me, "You can't open the gate because it's already open."

Humiliating? Wait, I haven't finished. He then walked over to tell the driver behind me that the problem was solved and I was on my way out, adding in a tone of voice not mean but simply explanatory: "The person driving that car is an elderly woman."

As I've already mentioned—despite my skinny black tights and adorable orange baseball cap—they can usually tell.

Sometimes we're treated like an elderly person. But sometimes we're treated as if we're not even there.

The writer Roger Angell, contemplating old age in his tenth decade, wanted it recognized that he was still here, ruefully noting that while "we elders have learned a thing or two," one of the things we've learned is "invisibility." He recalled a conversation with some of his younger friends—in their sixties—in the course of which, when there was a pause, "I chime in," contributing a few sentences that generate no reaction. None at all.

"The others look at me politely, then resume the talk exactly at the point where they've just left it. Hello? Didn't I just say something? Have I left the room?" He noted that he wasn't expecting to take over the conversation, "but I did await a word or two of response. Not tonight, though."

Angell observed that whenever he told this story to anyone around his age, he always got back smiles of recognition. "Yes, we're invisible. Honored, respected, even loved, but not quite worth listening to anymore. You've had your turn, Pops; now it's ours."

We women, as we grow older, often experience our own kind of invisibility, and by the Final Fifth it happens a lot. For the men who once let us know—in sometimes a coarse and sometimes a gentlemanly way—that they found us attractive definitely aren't into us anymore. No more appreciative glances, no more attentively hanging around, no more compliments or wolf whistles or passes. And while we might choose to attribute this restraint to the MeToo movement or general wokeness, we've observed that a lot of these men still retain and still express a hearty sexual interest—just not in old ladies.

Last month, while getting some shoes repaired, I and the store's owners, two sixtyish brothers, chatted comfortably while they did their work. Then a lovely young blonde walked into their shop. All of a sudden both of them, not one of them but both, were giving her their undivided attention—smiling, asking question about her vacation, telling her (in a nice way) how great she looked, while I, waiting patiently in my bare feet, had for all purposes totally disappeared.

"You've had your turn, Judy," I told myself. "Now it's hers."

It's hard to become invisible but it's also hard, we've learned, to be the recipients of too much attention, especially from our daughters and sons, who have bossily concluded that their folks are in need of some adult supervision.

They've taken to pointing out to us, while frowning at our cell, "There's 162 voicemails you haven't listened to." They've taken to pointing out to us, as they study and sniff the food we've stored in our frig, "There's stuff in there that died a year ago." In addition to which we have long been engaged in a no-end-in-sight intergenerational war—the War of the Car Keys. As in, "We think it's time that you stopped driving your car."

Car Wars may start with some joking remark like, "You almost hit that woman with the baby carriage. Want to take a right and try again?" Or, "Is there some special reason you've parked in the middle of the street and not at the curb?" Or some other comic routine which a daughter or son may mistake for a really witty first move. We are not moved.

We have, however, been noticing, though we'd rather not tell our kids, that we've recently been involved in a few minor accidents, all of which—though admittedly our fault—were, it's worth repeating, extremely minor. Like gently scraping the fender of a parked car. Like barely breaking the taillight of a car. Like backing out of a parking space and slowly backing into a moving car, whose horn was frantically beeping but which I wasn't able to hear because all my car windows were closed and I was listening to Vivaldi on the radio.

Since only the last of those accidents was mine, I have not felt any need to relinquish my car keys. Instead I have learned from experience and now, when I'm backing out, I always open the windows and turn off the radio. My other concessions to driving while old are stopping at every corner, whether or not I see a stop sign there. And when I have to turn left on a busy street with no green arrow to protect me from an alarming on-slaught of traffic, I always go around the block instead. Plus I tend to drive a little below the speed limit (except when I'm driving a lot below the speed limit). And I never, ever send a text while driving, and not just because I don't know how to text.

Still, it seems that some of my sons—actually, maybe all of

my sons—felt the world would be safer if I stopped driving. (Which, fast-forward, I very maturely, and of my own free will, have recently done. It was the right decision, and I hate it!)

To be perfectly fair, my sons also believed that I too would be a lot safer if I stopped driving. Safety, I have observed, is much on the minds of the children of us who are old. Which is why Milton grumbled in his later eighties that "my kids decided to confiscate my skis." Which is why, a friend gripes, "my daughter insists I give away all my high heels before, not after, I trip and break my neck." Which is why our kids are delighted that all the stoves in our RC are electric, not gas, "so you won't by mistake asphyxiate yourself." And which also is why every one of us is pestered by our children to wear a pendant or watch that will sound an alarm and summon help when we fall down. (Please notice that the word is "when," not "if.")

Now we're not denying it might be wise to install certain safety measures. But WE prefer to decide the what, when, and where. We don't want to lose any further say over our destiny. Like Roger Angell and all of us who are part of the Final Fifth, we want it recognized that WE'RE STILL HERE.

But it's not so easy to always feel WE'RE STILL HERE. And not only because of the ways that we're perceived and treated by others, but because of the ways we perceive and constrain ourself.

We may, for instance, put limits on where we go, how we look, what we do because we think our age makes such things inappropriate. Wearing a dress that shows off our breasts (though they still might deserve showing off) is inappropriate. Cha-cha-cha-ing too zealously—inappropriate. Trying to sound cool and with-it by using words like "cool" and "with-it"—inappropriate. Having sex with a person to whom we are or aren't married—definitely, embarrassingly inappropriate.

There are also things we're not doing even though we once loved doing them because they are, or we think they are, too hard. We did not get another dog when our last dog died. We're not cooking a Julia Child gourmet dinner for ten. We're not taking a walk in the snow when it's snowing outside. But the biggest thing we're not doing is traveling again, because we're finding traveling too hard. I've said it myself and I've heard it from so many Final Fifth friends: we don't want to travel because it's too damn hard.

Hanging on "hold" to make reservations—too hard. Dragging a carry-on suitcase through airports—too hard. Security lines and check-in counters—too hard. Seats that accommodate just half a tush—too hard. Middle seats and unhappy babies—too hard. And once we get where we're going—which is rarely, these days, on time—we are finding both our jet lag and mattress too hard.

We're finding travel too hard because our patience,

these days, isn't what it used to be. Our back—slipped disc, stenosis—is not what it used to be. And the energy that once allowed us to sightsee all day without desperate need of a nap is merely a weary fraction of what it used to be. And here, from a few more friends, are a few more reasons why Final Fifth folks say travel's too hard:

"I'm finding new places too confusing to navigate."

"No hotel is as nice as my house and my bed."

"We used to go to Maine but we can't get where we go by plane, and we've both stopped driving."

"When you feel you need a vacation to recover from your vacation it's time to stay home."

Even those who choose the easy comforts of a cruise ship, skipping the expeditions and settling into a deck chair instead for a nice long snooze, may regret signing up for that cruise when a sudden twinge in their chest has them asking, "Is this indigestion or a coronary?" Sometimes to be followed by the even more anxious question, "Is there a way to be airlifted to a hospital?"

Many of us have stopped traveling because we don't want to be that far from our doctors and hospitals.

And our world may start feeling smaller as we put away our

passports and our luggage, and decide staying home is what we prefer to do. And as we forsake Dulles Airport for the waiting rooms of our multiplying specialists, perhaps we've started feeling smaller too.

(Especially when they put us in one of those white paper dressing gowns, which close in the back—but our backside keeps peeking through, and we're steeling ourself for some dire diagnosis.)

Now I seem to remember a time when we knew more recipes for chicken than the names and phone numbers of our various "ologists." Of our cardi, endocrin, retin, and diabetologists. Of our dermat, radi, neur, and gynecologists. Our days are never empty because there is always some part of our body requiring an ologist's appointment. And as long as our aging body gives us good reason to complain, we won't be running out of conversation.

From knee replacement to skin biopsy to shots in the eye for macular degeneration, from arterial stents to a pacemaker in our chest, from chemotherapy and radiation to test after test after test after test after test, our bodies need help as they've year by year declined. But old age seems to be an equal opportunity assaulter, attacking not just the body but also the mind. Looking around the RC we start to notice that some of the residents aren't quite as sharp as they used to be, though many are highly accomplished retired professionals who can boast of a published book or a PhD. For there does seem to come, with aging, some mental slippage.

We've all, in fact, doubtless had some mental slippage. Then perhaps a little more slippage. Then maybe more. And then, for those with some really serious slippage, a move to a different building, a different floor. They're no longer a part of our RC's Independent Living community. And we're sad for them—and worried for ourselves.

All of us, by our fifth-fifth of life, have known or currently know spouses and parents, acquaintances and dear friends assailed with extreme to minimal mental diminishment, from Alzheimer's (whose brutal assault on a person's very self can look like *Invasion of the Body Snatchers*) to mild to moderate cognitive impairment (which, at its milder end, can, with some safety measures, allow those afflicted to maintain their independence). All of us also experience our own increased episodes of memory lapses, with the names of people and places or the location of valuable files vanishing for hours or days before they deign to make their reappearance. To those panicked folks who, at the first hint of memory failure, rush to their doctors asking, "Is this Alzheimer's?" one doctor offers this wise and consoling reply: "No, you don't have Alzheimer's; what you have is a slowing down of how your brain functions. Just as you have slowed down in your walking, so your brain has slowed down in the pace at which it processes information." Therefore, he adds, "It's important to be patient."

Still, observing someone forgetting their best friend's name, or where they're going, or what point—when they started their sentence—they wanted to make—may prompt us to brood about our own mental acuity. And sometimes we may find ourself engaged in some worrisome dialogue with . . . ourself:

What does it mean that I keep misplacing my glasses?
(Doesn't everyone?)

What does it mean I don't know where my hearing aids are?
(Just checked my ears—and here they are!)

And what does it mean that I spent an hour searching all over the parking garage for my car?
(I'm still convinced that somebody moved my car.)

And furthermore:

What does it mean that I'm wearing two different shoes?
(I need better lighting in the bedroom.)

And kissed a person I thought was—but wasn't—my son?
(Who says I thought he was my son?)

And what does it mean that the meat loaf I put in the oven an hour ago still isn't done?
(That happens a lot when I don't turn on the oven.)

Lying awake in our bed as the hands of the clock tick-tock relentlessly toward three, we're wondering, Are we beginning to . . .We're wondering, Are these symptoms of . . .We're wondering, Do we act like we're . . .We're wondering, Could we possibly be losing it?

Losing It

I know that I'm not, but I worry a lot about losing it.

I'm sure it's a fact that my mind is intact, but still . . .

In looking around I've found that some formerly fit folks

Suddenly seem to be on their way over the hill.

There's the friend, for example, who's meeting me at the
    right place but

She's on the wrong floor, or she's got the wrong day, or
    worse,

She's phoning to ask where I am and if, when I get there,

I maybe could help her to find her disappeared purse,

Which has doubtlessly disappeared because . . . she is losing
    it,

While I, I keep telling myself, have grey cells to burn,

Though I once knew the names of all of the Andrews
    Sisters,

And the only one I have for you now is LaVerne.

But I won't be conceding I'm needing to give up my car
keys.

So what, when I stop at a light, I take a short rest.

For I'm able to count by sevens back from one hundred—

If only they'd give me more time to finish the test:

Ninety-three, eighty-six, um—seventy-nine. Hey, who's
losing it?

I make lists: CHECKS TO WRITE. CLOTHES TO
CLEANERS. FOOD TO BUY,

Which then are combined into one comprehensive LISTS
LIST.

Forget to pay Comcast? Come home without milk? Not I!

Plus I have a few tricks to help fix short-term memory
meltdowns:

If my toothbrush is damp, I know I've already brushed.

A glance in the mirror tells me if I've combed my hair yet.

A glance in the toilet tells if I have indeed flushed.

I have also embraced that stern warning to use it or lose it,

Which is why I'm reciting state capitals a lot,

And all of the presidents, minus (oops!) Millard Fillmore,

And hoping that I can hang on to what I've still got,

And—seventy-two, sixty-five, fifty-eight, fifty-one—

(Wait! Have I already counted fifty-one?)

Trying to make the best of what's left of the rest of it.

What's Left

I don't want to flunk old age. I really want to be good at old age. If they're giving out grades for old age I want an A-plus. But we won't be good at old age until we've figured out what's left after we've dealt with a host of cascading losses. And perhaps among these losses the most difficult for us is the death of a husband or wife, who—for better and worse—has been part of our life for most of our lifetime.

I think we need a book entitled *Preparations for Widowhood*, and we need to read it BEFORE our husband dies. We also have plenty to learn from those who are widowed, much of it obvious, some of it a warning word to the wise that such-and-such should be said or done RIGHT NOW, while he's alive, because later is nonnegotiably too late.

Having some separate interests, some separate friendships, some separate sense of who we are, when who we are is not a part of a pair, can help to ease the separateness of widowhood. And we shouldn't wait till his death to figure out how to be a person, not only a wife. And we shouldn't be as pathetically clueless as I have always been about the practicalities of life, while my husband paid the bills, got the cars inspected, got us insured, did the taxes, and knew where all our important records were stored, and knew, when a pipe sprang a leak and water was spewing all over the floor, which valve to turn off. But although, in the security of my sensible safe RC, the management deals with the valves and replaces the dishwasher, there are many unfamiliar and highly uncongenial tasks waiting for me, tasks that I am frantically now learning how to do because Milton is no longer here to do them.

In addition we might consider, while he's still alive to hear them, making a few appropriate apologies, apologies for things we wish we had or hadn't done, apologies we owed but didn't make, apologies for a major failure or even a small insensitive mistake, like laughing instead of comforting him when he broke his big toe kicking the front door open.

What we also should think about doing—because we'll only be able to do it before, not after—is becoming more generous with a laugh, with a smile. Kissing him on the top of his head as we're passing, or even pinching his ass if that's our style. Hugging him with an all-out no-holds-barred hug. Or perhaps just reaching out and taking his hand. It's time to understand that we only have a little while longer to be together, and need, by word and by deed, to keep saying, "I love you."

*

If we can come to widowhood with more practical competence and fewer regrets, we'll be better prepared to make the best of the rest of it.

And after he's dead, it's helpful if we're also prepared for the not-that-remote possibility that some of us widowed might go a little bit nuts. Joan Didion relates, in her painfully beautiful book, *The Year of Magical Thinking*, how she couldn't give away her dead husband's shoes because—or so her bereaved logic went—what would he wear on his feet when he returned? My friend Kenny, among the most down-to-earth, nonmystical people I know, insists his dead wife came to visit him twice, standing behind his chair and caressing his neck. And many widows and widowers may live for months with the strangely persuasive sensation that their spouse isn't dead but merely in the next room.

My version of "a little bit nuts" was building a small shrine in Milton's home office, not a shrine to be worshipped at with candles and with prayers but . . . just a nice shrine. It has photos, one among many of the political books he wrote, his beloved coffeepot (now holding flowers), his favorite denim jacket, his press credentials, and various other markers of his energetic and most productive life.

(Oh, and along with my shrine I also have conversations with him from time to time—but I'll get to that later.)

*

The death of a spouse is usually life-transforming. Most manage to make a new life, but others will—like the wife of the late, great poet Dylan Thomas—see their future as "leftover life to kill." And some will look around in utter confusion and bewilderment, wondering why their previous life has vanished.

I'm thinking of Peg, whose husband was a man of much power and influence in Washington, and who shared with him an exciting life among the movers and shakers of D.C., some of whom she delusionally came to count among her dearest friends. And then her husband died, and almost at once the music stopped and the party was over.

"I just don't understand," she once complained to me, "why I never hear from anyone anymore. No dinner parties, no phone calls, no lunches, no weekends at their country place or the shore—what's going on here?"

Didn't she know, I asked, that she had belonged to that part of Washington where people related to people by their labels, and socialized with them because of their labels, and courted their spouses because they were married to labels? Wasn't she aware that these relationships, though interesting, even dazzling, were never really personal, never real? Didn't she understand that the deal was enjoy the heady scene, but don't count on it for anything important? And if your husband, the one with the label, dies, don't expect to count on it for anything.

But it turned out she wasn't prepared for this abandonment. And she wasn't prepared to make a different life. The last I heard, she had moved back to the little town she came from fifty years ago, not sure who she was anymore, now that she no longer was the wife of.

For a different kind of widowhood, there's ninety-year-old Sally, who has more than earned an A-plus in old age, putting together a life for herself that's allowed her to bloom and grow after her deeply beloved husband had died. A life that she has embraced although she still only sleeps on "her" side of the bed. A life fully lived by a woman who, for the first time in her life, is living alone, and:

Beginning her day with word games she plays by herself. Ending her day playing word games on Zoom with her grandchildren. Writing a family memoir. Making art in her home studio. Reading George Eliot. Taking a course in Graham Greene.

Visiting friends in nursing homes and rehab. Exercising and faithfully counting her steps. Going to movies and plays and art museums and memorial services and poetry readings. Going to yet another memorial service.

Connecting with family and friends over lunches and dinners. Connecting through intimate walks and talks on the phone. Enjoying a glass of wine at a cocktail party. Enjoying a glass of wine in her kitchen alone.

And though, like all the rest of us, she has family and health and a-leak-in-the-ceiling concerns, and though she misses her husband every day, and though—like me—she shares the gloomy foreboding that the world is on its way to Apocalypse Now, she knows how to laugh, and she knows how to love, and she knows that we'd all feel much better if we just sat down and read, or reread, *Middlemarch*.

Li is another woman who has earned an A-plus in old age after working—for decades, both in and out of government—on behalf of social justice, health care, and kids, while always keeping a careful and caring eye on the growing needs of her now-dead husband. She is a hearth of a woman, warming all of us who draw near, a hero dressed in Eileen Fisher clothes, helping everyone—and I mean everyone she knows, or barely knows—by figuring out some way to make their life better.

Driving them places, running their errands, tracking a missing delivery over the phone, plus sitting with them in ERs and doctors' waiting rooms so they won't be left there worried and alone, plus listening to and comforting them and dropping off home-cooked meals, and being so gracious and openhearted doing all this that you almost feel you'd offend her by not asking.

With devoted children and grandchildren, and a host of new and old friends, and a current writing project about her family's experiences with Nazi Germany, Li's only concession to being in her nineties was giving up skiing a couple of years ago.

If I haven't talked much about widowers it's because, compared to widows, I meet far fewer of them, both out in the wider world and at the RC. And the widowers that I've known don't seem to stay widowers very long, often receiving—before they're returned from the cemetery—casseroles accompanied by friendly condolence notes from available women. But I do need to mention Alan, who with his wife—the love of his life— wrote the lyrics of many great songs we all know and adore, and who, since she recently died, has managed, almost without a pause, to keep on writing them. Curious, generous, optimistic, he's working every day, and says that it's his work that keeps him going. And while he remains unpartnered, his wife is somehow a continuing part of his life, as Alan—at age ninety-nine—is busily writing some lyrics for a new musical.

Women like Sally and Li and men like Alan, who loved and mourned and will always remember their spouse, have—in that spouse's absence—succeeded in flourishing in old age by expanding on deeply valued parts of themselves: Sally by her creative and intellectual pursuits; Li by taking care—as she did when she worked on Medicare legislation—of everyone she can possibly take care of; Alan by still being Alan, perhaps even more so. Others, however, may choose instead to investigate new aspects of themselves, doing something they've never done before. Like journalist I. F. Stone, who, late in life, learned ancient Greek, the better to write his book about Socrates. Or like Fauja Singh, who at ninety ran his first—but not his final—marathon.

Few will strive for such grand late-life achievements. But all of us—widows and widowers, married, divorced, never married—need a reason to open our eyes in the morning, need to make meaning in the fifth-fifth of our life.

Psychoanalyst Erik Erikson describes eight stages, starting at our birth, in the course of psychosocial human development, resulting—if all goes well—in our successively becoming trusting, autonomous, ready to take the initiative, and industrious, followed—if all keeps going well—by our next developing a sense of self, a capacity for intimacy, and a wish to give to others—generativity. And then, beginning at age sixty-five, there's Erikson's eighth and final stage—integrity, when we start summing up what we've done with our life and find some gratification in what we've accomplished.

All of this is a valuable way to think about human development, except—I was sixty-five TWENTY-NINE YEARS AGO. And how long can people look back on their accomplishments? And how do we plan to live between now and dead? In a paper on the aging adult, Dr. Venus Masselam proposes adding a new psychosocial stage, a stage that will take us to age ninety-five as we deal with the tasks and complexities of late life. I see this as a stage where we'll work both on coming to terms with death and on making meaning in our life right now.

Making meaning may be, as it is with Alan and Sally and Li, doing more and more of what we love. Or it may be doing something completely new, but probably closer to tap-dancing than to marathons. Or it may be—and this is another legitimate choice—choosing to do nothing much at all.

For while there are folks in their Final Fifth whose lives are overflowing with activities, not everyone can, or wishes to, live that way, choosing instead to do little more compelling than smelling the roses, opting for a quieter, snoozier, undemanding, rock-in-a-rocking-chair life.

Some who once were the star of the show, possessed of a dazzling résumé, widely admired for all that they'd achieved, may be content, in their Final Fifth, to do without that attention and esteem, happy to have done what they did when they did it, and happy not to be doing it anymore.

Judy R is one of those superstars.

Judy, the former chief of child psychiatry at the National Institute of Mental Health, part of the National Institutes of Health, achieved international fame for her work in hyperactivity, obsessive-compulsive disorder, and the study and treatment of childhood schizophrenia. She has won more honors and prizes and produced more publications than I can find the space to document here. After a very long and distinguished career, she decided in 2017 to retire. She was, at the time, eighty-four years old!

And, she replies to my question, she doesn't miss it—not the work or the adulation. "I had done everything I wanted to do professionally. There was nothing that I needed to do anymore."

She moved to our RC with Stanley, her husband of sixty-plus years, who is also a retired NIH scientist, and has never thought, "Oh my goodness, what am I doing?" Instead, she sleeps till eleven and when she awakens, "I look forward to my day," reading, watching the news and maybe a movie, "while Stanley is very happily doing everything. And I'm very happy for Stanley to do everything."

In good weather on sunny Sundays, they drive to a pleasant restaurant by the Potomac and spend three midafternoon hours on its terrace, sharing a snack and watching the world go by.

"I could do this," she says dreamily, "for the next twenty Sunday afternoons with Stanley."

She means it.

For she has, without regret, let go of what used to be. She is enjoying who and where she is right now. This is a woman making the best of the rest of it. This is a woman at peace in her fifth-fifth of life.

At whatever pace we're living our life, all of us will endure the loss of many people that we love—not only our spouses but also our family and friends; that's why Sally goes to all those memorial services. The group photograph in our head has ever-more pictures of the dead, and as the English poet John Donne has famously said, "Any man's death diminishes me." And while I'm not in agreement that *any* death, anyone's death, really diminishes me—I can think of some where the opposite would be true—we certainly feel the loss when those who had mattered in our lives are increasingly absent. We will feel their loss, but some of those we've lost are going to leave us, before they go, with some powerful, unforgettable lessons in living.

My husband left me a powerful lesson in living.

For I watched this former skier, swimmer, and fearless journalist, who once traveled all over the world for a good story, learning a whole new way to live in his body. Beset by his wobbly imbalance, which still put him at risk for bad falls, and that stubborn arthritis in his foot, which eleven—eleven!—doctors couldn't remedy, he bit by bit by bit relinquished a physically active life for a short, cautious stroll with a friend plus a cane or a walker. Though he couldn't walk long and he would never walk again without pain, he did the best he could do with that cane and that walker!

But Milton had to adapt to a far harder change. He was slowly, but all too steadily, going blind, with a nonmalignant brain tumor doing damage to one of his eyes and macular degeneration to the other. He became barely able to read, so every morning I read him the *Washington Post* and *New York Times*, and Audible read him histories, mysteries, *War and Peace*, Chekhov, and other ennobling fare, and his truly amazing friend Michael was always ready to show up here to read him some provocative magazine article. With all of us stuffing his head with all of this reading matter, he might have been one of the best-read people in town, but he frequently had to close his eyes, lean back in his chair, or lie down because his compromised hearing made hearing exhausting.

He often had to take naps several times a day because the effort to live his life was exhausting.

"I'm a mess," he used to say as he considered his nap-filled days, his limited walks, and his nonstop doctors' appointments; plus the glasses he spilled or broke on his way to the kitchen; plus the movies—often too blurry, too mumbled, too British for him to follow on TV. He also bemoaned the fact that he kept on getting up at night "too many times; too damn many times" to pee.

And that was the full extent of Milton's complaining.

He complained now and then, but mostly he accepted and enjoyed his diminished but somehow still-satisfying life. He knew how to find satisfaction—he knew how to make meaning in his life.

He loved his sons and his daughters-in-law and his grand-kids. When I wasn't being a pain in the butt he loved me. He savored good meals, good friends, good conversation. And though, let me repeat, he barely could see, he maintained his independence by insisting on making the coffee and doing the dishes.

And we watched the news on CNN. And we listened to Leonard Cohen and Frank Sinatra. And we cuddled on the couch. And we talked and talked.

We talked about climate change, Russia, guns, and the children. We talked about the market—leave or stay? We never discussed the Kardashians or TikTok—or what he wanted the words on his tombstone to say. He lived as if there would be another day, and another day, and another day. Though he'd lost a lot in this Final Fifth of his life, he was doing his best with what was left of the rest of it. He was doing his best with the rest till the day he died.

I'm giving Milton an A-plus in old age.

Making the best of what's left will have many different defini-tions. For some what's most important is being paired. There are late-life widows and widowers who find that life unpart-nered has lost its savor. There's no one to sleep in their bed at night, or discuss the news over breakfast, or make them feel that it matters that they're there. They've got places to go and things to do; they've got family and they've got friends. But even with plenty of plenty, it's not enough. Their definition of meaningful is to share the rest of their life in intimate connec-tion with another. This need overrides all other considerations.

And of course there will be other considerations: Like how many years will the two of them have together? What late-life tribulations will have to be shared? And since one of them in-evitably will face the death of a partner once again, are they willing to do it again? Are they really prepared to once more endure the losing and the leaving?

But the chance to be loved and touched and seen and heard and singled out may prove irresistible, imperfect though it's probably going to be. As the sky turns grey and the days keep getting shorter, it's tempting to ask "grow old along with me."

Grow Old Along with Me
and My Home Health Aide

Grow old along with me and my home health aide.

Let's merge our meds and be each other's dear.

I'll nudge you when you haven't zipped your zipper.

You'll help me hook the hooks of my brassiere.

You'll get to tell your new-to-me old stories.

(I can't complain I know each one by heart.)

I'll try to listen without interrupting.

You'll try to leave the room before you fart.

Perhaps we'll both be slightly better versions

Of what we both had let ourselves become

Through married life's eruptions and incursions.

Perhaps we've grown more grateful and less dumb,

And quicker with a "sorry" and a "yes, dear,"
And slower to take umbrage than to smile.
Or none of the above. But nonetheless, dear,
Grow old along with me a little while.

A Little While

A little while was all the time that Anna and Walter had—their love story ended almost before it started. And the few of us who knew about it were practically as brokenhearted as they. For what happened to them was a late-life almost-fairy-tale that failed to deliver its happily ever after, one of the major risks when people fall in love in the Final Fifth of their life.

This long-term widow and widower had journeyed from D.C. neighbors . . . to comfortable, casual, let's-get-together companions . . . to, as Anna ruefully put it, "an actual return-to-the-living romance." Two openhearted people with many accomplishments and good works, with well-launched adult children and sufficient shared interests to brighten this new phase of life, they had just begun to explore the sweet possibilities of an upper-eighties love affair when he suffered a quite devastating fall. Confined to a wheelchair, barely able to speak, unable to meet any physical needs on his own, Walter—his mind and warmth and essential Walterness still intact—is now cared for by full-time attendants under the supervision of a devoted daughter, with Anna paying brief visits a few times a week.

"I've been able to take the role of a caring friend," is how she explains her current status, though sustained conversations are difficult and sometimes she worries her visits make him sad. Sitting there holding his hand, she hopes he's not troubled by painful thoughts of what might have been. Sitting there holding his hand, she has firmly put away any dreams of fairy-tale endings.

Love, in the final years of life, can certainly be a significant source of happiness. But it rarely is a fairy tale. Or a dream come true. Or a many-splendored thing. For newly partnered couples there will likely be a period of adjustment as irritating attitudes and habits and limitations come to light, requiring allowances to be made and compromises to be negotiated. But even long-married couples will find that major adjustments are needed as love's definition begins to include some necessary dealings with their own and each other's mental and physical difficulties. Along with the really big ones—cancer, heart disease, and stroke, and let's add dementia and devastating falls—there's often the winding down in late life of mobility, sexuality, mental acuity, hearing and sight, accompanied by—despite a deep commitment to sunblock and yoga—the wrinkling and shrinking of the human body. Furthermore, those who have downsized from a house to an apartment in an RC and are living with less privacy and less space may confront far more assaults on their sensibilities, including unsought encounters with her leak-proof pantiliners and his stool softener. It seems that love in the later years, whether long-standing or new, may require more Metamucil and less fastidiousness.

Love, in a marriage's later years, may also present a wife with the necessity of becoming her husband's caretaker. And while husbands have also commendably been the caretakers of their wives, I've mostly heard tales of the other way around. (Perhaps because women tend to live longer than men, and also because, traditionally, women have been assigned the caretaking role.) Yet even with full-time home health aides, some of the kindest and most competent wives I know have discovered how hard it is to take care of a husband. A husband who really hates being taken care of, or told what to do.

Connie's husband, Gary, whose last five years of life were increasingly beset with physical and cognitive impairments, especially hated being told what to do. Exercise? "I don't feel like it. Don't bug me. Leave me alone." Hearing aids? "Don't want them. Don't need them. I am hearing fine." He also, after reluctantly enduring a hearing test, forbade the audiologist to tell his wife, who'd accompanied him, the results. And so the audiologist, respecting the rules of confidentiality, said not a word to Connie but conveyed her diagnosis by silently bobbing her head in an up-and-down "yes."

Nobody ever persuaded him to get hearing aids.

Nor could Connie ever persuade him to exercise. Or (till she got outside help) to quit driving his car. Or to do any of the things he'd been warned he needed to do for his safety or health.

"I urged, I suggested, I'd talk about some article I pretended I had read, or make up some story I'd claim that someone had told me," all for the purpose of coaxing him into compliance. She finally gave up.

But though Gary was becoming more and more out of it, he enjoyed joining Connie to dine with mutual friends, trying hard to keep up with the conversations. And she'll always remember his turning to her after a night when he'd managed to hold his own, and proudly saying, "I put on a good show, didn't I?" Words that could make you laugh. Or make you cry.

Catherine had to deal with a quite unusual caretaking issue. Her husband, Seth, was suffering from a particularly distressing form of dementia, which included his developing the perplexing, unnerving delusion that Catherine wasn't actually his wife. This led to a lot of strife, like his refusing to share his bed with this imposter, till the matter was resolved quite happily. For Seth, having gradually grown attached to this caring, attractive stranger, asked her to marry him. Catherine accepted with alacrity. And with an exchange of new wedding rings, and a modest ceremony and champagne reception, they pledged to be husband and wife all over again.

Harriet's husband, Jason, suffered through eight cruel years of Parkinson's and dementia, beginning with denial, and moving on to explosive rage, and ending in bleak resignation and long silences. Harriet was with him each step of the way. During his denial stage, while he still was going to work, she had to help him button his shirt every morning, a task, it was tacitly understood, that had to be accomplished with no explanation, a lot of pretend nonchalance, and "neither of us ever acknowledging he needed help." As the full impact of his dementia had this once soft-spoken man screaming some version of "Why has this happened to me?" Harriet was often the object of his frustration and anger, some of which—though she kept reminding herself it wasn't his fault—made her cry. Jason's death, for Harriet and for all of us who loved him, was both a release and a still-continuing loss.

Unlike Connie, Catherine, and Harriet, whose husbands have died, Marna—with the help of three excellent 24/7 caretakers—still lovingly watches over her husband, Larry, whose Parkinson's had been followed by a stroke which, since 2016, has left him unable to talk and completely paralyzed. Settled here a few years ago, Marna greets Larry each morning with a kiss, a cheery "Hello, handsome husband," and a heartfelt "Do you know how much I love you!" And she remains convinced that, after fifty-plus years of marriage, they are still in some meaningful way in touch with each other, that—"I can always tell by that little puckering of his forehead"—he is still sometimes able to take in and "get" what she says.

Marna says of their relationship before all the bad stuff struck, "He loved me the way I needed to be loved." The tender gratitude with which she quietly speaks these words is a promise that she will watch over him forever.

Many caretaking wives devote themselves to improving their husband's life by taking them from doctor to doctor in search of pain relief, or better control of symptoms, or maybe even the miracle of a cure. They're also there to ask questions and follow-up questions, and to carefully (how do you spell that?) write down the answers, and maybe even to (tactfully) mention a promising new treatment that a friend of a friend is getting and how come their husband's not getting that treatment too? Not all of our husband's doctors were crazy about us.

(Note: I found that, during the many months I was taking Milton to doctors, I had absolutely no interest in writing anything. Although I'd been writing and sending out poems since I was seven years old, I suddenly found myself with nothing to say.

And while I was concerned about the vanishing of this basic part of myself, I was struck with what a relief it was to—not for a minute—be pulled in two directions: take care of my husband or sit at my desk and write. This experience made me think about how often women are torn by a sometimes exhausting array of conflicting demands—the marriage, the children, the job, the book-group reading—and how luxurious it was—the children grown, the writing paused, the book unread—to focus, unconflicted, on just one thing. This absence of ambivalence, to my surprise, had the effect of lightening my life.)

While I, and many friends of mine, cared for our husbands responsibly, this doesn't mean we were always on good behavior. There's a certain slippage of manners and grace in the course of a long-term marriage, and becoming our husband's caretaker doesn't help, especially when we find ourselves behaving like nags and nannies and enforcers. The erosion of romantic illusion inevitably accelerates as we go from man and wife to man and the person who laces his orthopedic boot and scrapes the wax from his clogged hearing aids. And when those of us who were scraping off wax and lacing up that damn boot are now filling out forms where our marital status is "widow," are we willing to open our heart to love again?

Are we ready for a relationship? A new romantic relationship? A new romantic physical relationship? A relationship that involves taking off our clothes? A late-in-life relationship where the bloom is indisputably gone from the rose?

Catherine says an unequivocal yes!

Wrung-out after spending the last seven years of a long and contented marriage tenderly tending a husband with deep dementia, she found herself being courted—after his death—by an old acquaintance, Eddie, a zesty widower who was full of fun and joy. He first won over her four adult children by taking them out to dinner "to meet the guy who's crazy about your mother," and then moved into her heart and into her bed. And until his recent death at age ninety-three, they enjoyed six years of travel and golf, shared families and shared friends, along with a sweet and loving "little while."

Eddie has said of his late wife, Sandy, and Catherine's late husband, Seth, that this, "our relationship, was their last gift to us. Because both of us had such happy marriages with them, we are able to have this new happiness with each other."

Dina, widowed for almost a decade after a long, good marriage, didn't like being a widow but made do, "putting on a happy face" and busily filling her days with friends and family and reading, and her work as a thriving literary agent. She and her husband had been close friends with Matthew, one of his partners, and his wife, a friendship that lasted after her husband died, a deep and enduring friendship which continued after Matthew's wife also died, a deep and enduring and warm and caring friendship that one might not wish to disrupt with romantic feelings.

Then Dina started having romantic feelings.

One night, deciding to risk it, she gathered her courage and said to Matthew, "What if I said I had designs on you." To which, without hesitation, he enthusiastically answered, "That would be the most wonderful moment of my life."

So now they're living together—"together forever," Dina says, and she's mad about Matthew, who "thinks that I am wonderful." He also, says Dina, "thinks that it's his job to make me laugh," so there's always a lot of laughter around their house. They've also learned a lesson or two, some of them very painful, over the many years of their earlier marriages, lessons that have allowed them to better complement and take care of one another. Dina has evolved from a 1950s stay-at-home college-dropout mommy to a competent, confident woman with advanced degrees and a very successful career (to which she adds, " I'm also a kinder person"). Matthew comes to Dina having made peace with some difficult issues from his past life. (And he's working on being a less impatient person.) Both of them into their nineties and blessed with good health as well as each other, they're "committed to making the most of our final years," says Dina. "Falling in love was a wonderful surprise." And whatever time remains to them, they're grateful to be growing old together.

Fixed up by mutual friends, Katie and Charles—she long divorced, he recently widowered—knew they were meant for each other on their first date, after talking nonstop until they had closed the restaurant. Soon after they met, however, he developed some worrisome symptoms which, if what they feared turned out to be true, would be the signs of a cruel and fatal disease.

In which case, a heartbroken Charles told Katie, they'd go their separate ways. He wouldn't put her through this tortuous endgame. Their story—so full of promise—would be done.

Katie listened quietly as Charles readied her for a possible goodbye, then answered him with two small words: "Too late." They loved each other too much, the connection between them already unbreakable. Leaving him? Unthinkable! It was too late.

And thanks to a kindly fate, it joyfully wound up not too late for them to have several happy years together.

In several of the second-chance-at-happiness stories I've heard there are concerns about having fallen in love too soon, with expressions of fear that the outside world would regard the recent widower or widow as callous, disloyal, or insensitive for so rapidly replacing their dead mate, and hoping—when out with their new love on a date—to not run into anyone they know. Roger Angell dismissed such concerns.

Instead he wrote that he and his wife "didn't quite see the point of memorial fidelity," sharing the view that when one of them died, the other should find someone else without wasting a moment. Whoever died first would know, they believed, that he or she would keep being loved forever, while the one who was left behind, they believed, should quickly remarry, recouple, reconnect. We "oldies," he said, deeply yearn for connection.

For the biggest surprise of his life, wrote Angell, who became a widower in his early nineties, "is our unceasing need for deep attachment and intimate love," our yearning for domesticity, companionship, conversation, a familiar body to nestle with in the night. Whatever our age, if we lose this, he wrote, we will never lose our longing for its return. And "if it returns, we seize upon it avidly."

It's no surprise, however, that not all new late-life couples (including some that have lasted for several years) wind up being happy. Two women I know have been willing to tolerate difficult relationships because they can't bear to live alone, or without the validation of a man. In Zelda's case, her live-in partner is universally loathed by all her friends, who beg her to leave him home when they get together. (And Zelda herself doesn't seem to like him much either.) And the three men that have serially populated Stella's widowhood have been: meanly hypercritical; scarily controlling; and poorly matched intellectually and sexually.

I've talked to very-glad-to-be-coupled new couples, some of whom met in the world outside the RC, others whose fateful encounter was maybe right here, at the Current Events Discussion Group. I've also talked to widows who have told me quite decisively that they have no interest in another relationship. "I was happy—very happy—to take care of *my* old man," explained Elizabeth. "But I have no wish to take care of anyone else's."

Aside from a reluctance to sign up as the caregiver in a new relationship, women, and men, may find other reasons after their partner is gone to choose to live their final years alone, concerned with clashing views on where to live and how to live, with political differences and financial disparities, and—a BIG ONE—the failings and intrusions of his and her adult children, not all of whom would be thrilled to see a parent in a new romantic arrangement.

There are some adult children smart enough to be grateful for their mother's or father's new happiness, grateful there's someone besides themselves to provide it, and sometimes even grateful for the expanded and welcoming family that (if they've hit the jackpot) can be a bonus of this new relationship. There are also many far less lovely responses.

For some adult children are going to feel resentful, even abandoned, when a parent has a new love in his or her life. And some, who were hoping that *they* (symbolically speaking) would be their parent's new husband or new wife, will discourage, disparage, sabotage new relationships, before and during, and right to the bitter end.

Angell recalled a twice-widowed woman who found, in her eighties, another man to love, and they had, before his death, a few good years. After he died she arranged with his children to come to his house and pick up her belongings, unprepared for what was awaiting her there, and finding, when she arrived, all her belongings already lined up—outside the front door.

Another reason why some—though more widows than widowers—aren't all that eager for a new partner is that they've found they love living on their own, with no one to accommodate to, no one whose wishes and needs must be considered. They can read till two in the morning, they can eat dinner standing up, they can binge on any dumb series that they choose. "And there's something to be said," Laura says, "about having no one but you that you have to please."

On the other hand, says Katie, there is something to be said about having another wonderful relationship, but that would require another wonderful partner. The flourishing woman that she'd become in the course of her years with Charles feels no need of a mere companion today. "I can go to a concert or restaurant by myself, stay home by myself, take care of myself. I don't ever feel I have to be part of a couple. And our relationship was so loving in so many depths and dimensions that I don't think anything less could touch my heart."

There are those of us, however, who—though not in so idyllic a relationship—were married to someone who deeply touched our heart. We know just how good—when it's good— being married is. We were each other's shield against aloneness. He was our permanent person, and we were his. Ours were not easy marriages but messy, exhausting, intense—intimate, till-death-do-us-part entanglements.

Ah, entanglements.

I remember telling my women friends how much I always enjoyed it when Milton was away on a multi-week writing assignment, and I got to be the only boss of my life. "Of course you enjoy it," one of them once shrewdly said to me. "You get a little time-out from being a wife." And, she added, "you know he's coming home."

Except he won't be coming home anymore.

And I have no interest in starting again—with anyone, though I'm happy for and rooting for those who do. I don't want some Perfect Pete or Terrific Ted. I just want my imperfect Milton to stop being dead.

Stop Being Dead

I have these conversations with my husband.
I'm hoping that he's hearing what I've said.
For though I know he died this past December,
I keep on telling him, Stop being dead.

You've never been a stickler for the rules, dear.
You've crossed some lines—and some were really red.
Obedience is not among your virtues.
So stop obeying! Just stop being dead.

I need you sitting at our kitchen table.
I need you lying next to me in bed.
I need you fixing our damn circuit breakers.
I need you! Could you please stop being dead?

It's only you for whom I'm feeling lonely.
I won't take any substitutes instead.
Who knew you'd be completely irreplaceable?
Come back to me! Come back! Stop being dead.

Counting the Dead

Though he's probably not coming back to me, despite my repeated requests, I talk to my husband and think about him—a lot, especially late at night when I'm lying in bed. For instead of counting sheep when I have difficulty sleeping, it's become my habit to count and name the dead.

The dead I am counting are mine—my family and friends, my romantic friends and a few others—along with one public figure who has always felt like part of my personal history. In counting them and naming them, I'm remembering who they were—and were to me. I'm recalling the me I was then—and am no more. I'm wishing that I had done this, and hadn't done that, that I'd never been so young and so clueless. I'm learning some lessons I should have learned decades before. Counting and naming the dead has made me happy, sad, proud, embarrassed, angry, and grateful. It hasn't always provided a good night's sleep. But I've found that there are benefits in counting the dead instead of counting sheep—in this process of love and regret and rueful remembrance.

*

The first two dead I count and name—I was in my teens when they died—are my mother's difficult mother, Grandma Clara, and my up-to-then only president, FDR, over whom, to be perfectly honest, our family shed a lot more tears than we did for Clara. The reason I name Franklin Roosevelt and none of the other public heroes who died in my lifetime is that President Roosevelt (as I and so many Jews of my generation were raised to believe) knew us, understood us, cared about us—and in some undefined but encompassing way watched over us.

And I had proof!

It was 1940 and Bunny, who lived next door to me, was eager to mail off some holiday cards she had written. But Bunny was only eight, and the nearest mailbox was three highly trafficked streets away, and her parents—despite much argument from a deeply disgruntled Bunny—wouldn't let her walk there on her own. After she'd argued—and lost—her case, her father suggested, playfully I presume, that she take up the mailbox matter with President Roosevelt. And that was exactly what Bunny did, writing and mailing a letter straight to the top, seeking a solution to her problems with dangerous crossings and distant mailboxes. And not too long after her letter was sent, a new mailbox was installed—right down at the corner of our street.

Yes, FDR was benevolently watching over us. Grandma Clara, however, not so much. Indeed, the Clara I knew was a grouchy, testy fire hydrant of a woman, who lived with us for a while—a strenuous while, and who saw her role in our lives as complainer-in-chief and in-house critic, poor strategies for winning hearts and minds. Yet when I think of her now, when I lie in bed and name her name, I also remember the few things I knew about her: that she was widowed early; was left with no money, no skills, and four young children to raise; was urged but refused to give them up for adoption; and somehow—how I wish that I had asked her how she'd done it—brought up her daughters and sons to productive adulthood.

In naming the dead I am often troubled by questions I should have asked, questions that no one alive today can answer, questions that all of us should be asking the Claras in our life before it's too late. What was your life like when you were growing up? What did you think, or hope, your future would be? Why did you choose to marry the person you married? What was your biggest mistake? What accomplishments are you most proud of? What are some of your dearest memories?

Everyone, even difficult grandmas, has stories they'd like to tell, stories it could enrich our lives to hear. Among my biggest regrets are all the stories I never heard because I never thought to ask the questions.

Death, however, was much on my mind when I was growing up, and I wrote about it in poems of fatal intensity, poems that featured dead parents, entire dead families, dead soldiers, dead dogs, and—in late adolescence—a near-dead me:

Death and desire crumpled in a corner.
And I in black, the solitary mourner.
Often finale but birth, thank God, more often.
And yet I think I know too well the coffin.

My parents, reading my writings, recommended I write poems less and ride my bike more.

During my twenties I married, and then divorced, and then re-married, far too immersed in life to obsess about death, though I do remember telling a friend, whose grandfather had died, how lucky I felt to have made it through this decade without losing anybody that I loved. I should have, but didn't, knock on wood as superstition advises us to do when tempting fate with such provocative claims. But after what happened happened, I never ever failed to knock on wood again.

For when I was twenty-nine my husband, Milton, and I had a baby, our first baby, a baby boy who was born too soon and perished after only two days on this earth. I never held him or touched him, attached as he was to assorted tubes and drips and machines. And when I name him at night, when I acknowledge the brief existence of Jacob Anthony, I offer an apology for not once having taken him into my arms.

There weren't, and maybe still aren't, any ceremonies or rituals to mark the life and death of born-too-soon babies. So all I could do for a while, quite a while, was talk about it and cry about it to practically anyone who just said hello.

My first published writing on death was not one of my death-and-desire poems, but a children's book called *The Tenth Good Thing About Barney*. I wrote it when Tony, our oldest, was eight, in the wake of a quite daunting conversation.

"Mommy," Tony asked me one day, completely out of the blue, "am I going to die?"

"Everyone dies," I said briskly, as some child-raising book had recommended I do. "But you won't die for a very very long time."

After a thoughtful pause he came back with, "But do I have to die?"

"Everyone dies and you will too," I matter-of-factly repeated. "But not for a very very"—and I grew firmer with every very—"very very very VERY long time."

There was silence on the other end (while I prayed this would go away), after which Tony tearfully said to me, "Mommy, Mommy, I don't want to die."

And I, not able to bear my son's distress for another second, offered this desperate and utterly shameless reply: "Well, maybe they'll invent something."

After which I decided I needed some better answers on death—both for Tony and me.

In my Barney book a little boy is mourning the death of his cat and finds solace in recounting good things about him: that Barney was brave and funny and smart, and only once ate a bird, among several other—a total of nine—fine qualities. He is comforted too by learning that Barney, buried in the yard, will help grow the flowers, Barney's tenth good thing and "a pretty nice job for a cat."

Dealing with death through memories and through understanding we're part of the cycle of nature, that nothing that's part of nature is ever lost. Not my last word on the subject but surely a whole lot better than maybe they'll invent something.

Over the decades death became more frequent and more familiar, though sometimes still quite painfully premature.

I count my mother, Ruth—a warm and much-beloved woman—whose heart gave out just short of age sixty-three, who starred at tournament bridge, and knew every lyric of every song, and whose love of books made a reader and writer of me, and whose glorious gift for friendship, suffused with goodwill and empathy, taught me all I needed to know about friendship. Wreathed in cigarette smoke as they chatted in our breakfast nook or sun parlor, telling her secrets they could be sure she'd keep, my mother's Yetta and Pearl, and all the others she called "the girls," became the benevolent context of her life.

None of these women, including my mother, worked outside the home. None of them aspired to a career. Most of them were smarter, stronger, more patient, and better drivers than their husbands. But their job was to tend the house, raise the kids, have conjugal sex when required, and do some do-good work as a volunteer. Most were the daughters of immigrants and what they wanted above all else wasn't passion, love, adventure, or a PhD in physics. It was security.

(My mother's sister Florence actually chose to get a PhD in physics. But because she never married and had children, I was raised to believe that her life was a tragic failure.)

Security, as these women understood it, usually came from being someone's wife. They also understood that in the world and time they lived in, men made the money and women made the life, which meant that their husbands earned enough to support them (without, thank God, their having to get a job), and had bought enough insurance to leave them what was called "well fixed" in widowhood.

Though my mother died too soon to be a widow, her friends—enjoying their children, their grandkids, their card games, their swim clubs, their cruises, and each other—knew how to have a merry widowhood.

Maybe some of those Yettas and Pearls were women who

harbored larger, grander ambitions. Maybe, as a feminist friend once suggested, marriage—for some—was where dreams went to die. Maybe, for the wife who lived on Miltown, and the wife who saw a psychiatrist once a week, the price they paid for security was too high. And maybe it took me too long to consider the maybes.

My younger sister, Lois, like my mother, also died too soon to be a widow. As I name and think about Lois I remember a blue-eyed blonde with a Daisy Mae body, in every way the opposite of me—outdoorsy, athletic, interested in science, bored with Nancy Drew and poetry, yearning to go to medical school but, since she wasn't a boy and wouldn't be working too long before she got married, was pressed instead to become a lab technician.

Despite our differences Lois always yearned to be my best friend. I always yearned to be an only child. But twenty months after my birth I had to share my mother and father with this cuddly, roly-poly baby sister. I've spent half my life writing reams about sibling rivalry.

And in truth I wasn't what you'd call the sweetest and kindest big sister in northern New Jersey.

My sister had many gifts—the plants she planted always thrived; mine always withered. She was a gourmet cook, champion tennis player, great mom. But what I remember best is the remarkable strength and courage, the unyielding grace and dignity and calm, with which she faced her dying and death at fifty.

On Saturday afternoons, when we were kids, my sister and I would go to the movies. For twenty-five cents apiece we got quite a deal: Two feature films. A cartoon. A heart-stopping serial. The coming attractions. A news-of-the-week newsreel. And then the lights came on and the theater held its popular weekly yo-yo contest, with boys and girls competing up on the stage. And though I never came close to winning a contest, I never—until an embarrassingly advanced age—went to that movie theater without my yo-yo.

And I never got through a movie where, if an animal—any animal—was hurt, my sister didn't start sobbing noisily, requiring me to drag her out of her seat and into the lobby until she recovered. Untroubled by the massacres and mayhem afflicting the humans on the screen, she gave all her sympathy to the nonhuman creatures, invariably falling apart if a cowboy spurred his horse or a puppy's paw was stepped on. Mopping her dripping eyes and nose, and furious that I was missing part of the movie, I'd reproach my sister for being so wimpy and weak. I never dreamed that one day, mopping my dripping eyes and nose, I'd speak at her funeral—and call her the bravest person I'd ever known.

One night when I couldn't sleep I got out of bed and queried Google on why this God I staunchly don't believe in allows so much pain and suffering in the world. Google directed me to "The Book of Job." And there, when the much-abused Job has finished setting forth his complaints, God chooses to answer his questions with more questions:

"Where wast thou when I laid the foundations of the earth?"

"Knowest thou the ordinances of heaven?"

"Will the unicorn be willing to serve thee?"

"Shall he that contendeth with the Almighty instruct him?"

Despite these reminders of my insignificance, and despite the fact that I staunchly don't believe in Him, I find myself contendething a lot.

The next of my names is Abe, my sixteen-years-older-than-I first husband: My hero, my teacher, my major pain in the ass. Law professor until the dire days of McCarthyism. Eccentric delight of his legal philosophy class. Dabbler in tarot cards and Jewish mysticism. Fervent fisherman of bluefish and bass.

Unfaithful and contentious and impossible to live with, but a man who, after our quite uncontentious divorce, remained a dear and devoted friend until his untimely death at sixty-two.

Abe had been fired from Rutgers Law School for taking the Fifth Amendment, as many brave people in many professions had done, rather than answer questions from congressional committees about their political affiliations. But after the 1950s, when the witch hunt had finally begun to run its course, and some universities started to offer apologies to the teachers they had fired, Abe hoped he too would receive some public acknowledgment of the damage that had been done to him. He died without receiving that acknowledgment.

But I, along with Milton, pursued the matter, sporadically prodding Rutgers on Abe's behalf. And in 2009, more than half a century after I, a terrified twenty-two-year-old, helplessly sat in a hearing room, watching as her husband's career was destroyed, I held in my hands a letter—a heartfelt, beautiful, apologetic letter!—from the chancellor of Rutgers University–Newark.

It expressed "profound regret" at what had been done to Abe and two other Rutgers professors. It spoke with pain and sorrow of the "mistakes that were made," the "injustices" that had occurred. It called the firings "a blot upon our reputation." And although it was fifty years later and although Abe had long been dead, justice—imperfect, delayed—had had the last word.

"We did it," I sometimes say, when lying in bed and counting the dead, I speak Abe's name.

And I smile when I count and name my father, Martin, on his own from my mother's death until his late eighties, recalling

I had to notify three different ladies in three different states that their boyfriend (past, present, potential) would no longer be available for phone conversations, or dinner, or . . . fooling around. In naming him I'm remembering that my father loved women, loved ballroom dancing, loved golf, and hated the New York Yankees so passionately that, after his first heart attack, his doctor sternly told him that he could never watch the Yankees play again.

"Every time they win," said Dr. F, "your blood pressure goes straight through the roof. You're going to give yourself another coronary."

I also remember my father's unfailing embrace of his life-long duties as an accountant, or—as he liked to remind us—a CPA, never deterred by bad health or bad weather conditions from showing up at the office every day. And though I always credited my bookish mother for turning me into a writer, it's taken me much longer to see that what helped me become a deadline-meeting professional was my father's tush-on-the-seat-get-the-job-done work ethic.

With each new decade the names of the dead accumulate, accelerate. I count the names of my in-laws, Betty and Lou, good decent people who guarded their pennies, cherished their only son, had little talent for playfulness or pleasure, and who once, when they came to visit us from New Jersey, stood at our front door weeping because, they explained, they'd have to go home in a couple of days.

I could have been, and should have been, and very much wish I had been a more generous and more patient daughter-in-law.

As I count the dead, my couldas and shouldas besiege me: I should have sat with Clara and heard her stories. I should have held my baby before he died. I could have been a more welcoming sister to Lois, and not been such a meanie when she cried. I could have invited my in-laws to please come inside and stay a whole week instead of a weekend.

I could have made more room in my heart—and made more time in my life—for the people who came knocking at my door. I could have mustered more grace and more good humor as I barreled through my kids-career-marriage days. I could have treated my to-do list as something less, far less than a sacred document. And though I figured out some of this in time to mend my ways, the regrets I have to live with, I'll have to live with.

I count and name Milton, the sexy boy I met when we were eighteen and nineteen years old, and married—after some detours—ten years later.

I count the other men—romantic partners, special friends—who powerfully shaped the contours of my life.

Larry, tender and earnest—my first love.

David, who said I had brains—and urged me to use them.

Albert and Henry and Jack and Carl and Richard and Paul and Bert, who

. . . introduced me to Mondrian and Picasso.

. . . taught me the proper way to eat an artichoke.

. . . switched me from Doris Day to movies with subtitles.

. . . insisted (wrongly) that I could learn to play chess.

. . . took me to several lectures on World Federalism.

. . . took me to several lectures on Sigmund Freud.

. . . and encouraged me to become a stop-the-war, civil rights, women's rights political woman, marching in protests, chanting at rallies, waving signs at demonstrations, and picketing the White House (with one, then two, and finally three little boys in tow). I even got arrested a couple of times.

I also count and name the married men who became my friends as part of a couple, and who, along with their wives, were the companions of our lives, Milton's and mine—friends we dined with, traveled with, went to movies and concerts with, and celebrated life's major milestones with: Steve and Dan, on-the-side-of-the-angels journalists. Bob, whose elegant legal mind I revered. Peter, a playful pediatric surgeon, who sometimes cheered up his worried young patients by greeting them dressed up in a gorilla suit. And Leonard, an activist rabbi, committed to

social justice, world peace, and Major League Baseball, whose devoted congregation loudly and lovingly laid him to rest with a raucous rendition of "Take Me Out to the Ball Game."
I believe that each of these men, in his own way, would have hurried to help me had I called for help. And though I can't call on them anymore, I count them, and I name them, and I remember them.

And of course I count the women—my comforters, confidantes, gurus, playmates, soul mates, pals—without whom I'd have had an impoverished life: Two Judys, Phyllis, Sunny, Shay, Joy, and Elaine. Ruth C, Ruth G, Grace, Bonnie, Jean, and Kitty. Plus Polly, Sheila, Rhoda, and Saone. Plus Carol and Martha, Libby, Ellie, and Ann. They were therapists, artists, writers, fashion designers, economists, social workers, lawyers, actors, political activists, educators. They were wives and mothers and grandmas and volunteers. In naming them I remember our shared laughter, shared anxieties, shared tears; instructions in making a cheese soufflé, discussions about what's going on "down there"; Kitty's breathtaking brilliance; Shay's ferocious independence; Phyllis's awesome gift of empathy; Polly's patient guidance through the terrors of early motherhood; Ruth G trying to teach the twist to me. Our poetry group, our novels group, our lunch dates and walking dates and phone conversations. Our years and years of tea and sympathy.

And our trusting revelations about our marriages, kids, insecurities, work, and weight; about our transgressions, indiscretions, screwups—everything.

In religious memorial services, in Black Lives Matter shout-outs, on the anniversary of 9/11, in the news of how many the virus has killed today, there are many different ways, many different reasons, for us—the living—to count and name the dead. I do it because it allows me to honor their memory and our shared history. It deepens my understanding of who they were, what we meant to each other. It shows me what, even now, I might try to repair. It is, I suppose, the closest I get to prayer. And in its rue and regret, as well as in its many sweet recollections, it enriches my life.

And one thing more.

As a lifelong nonbeliever my version, my vision, of immortality is being remembered by others after death. And although, once people die, they're likely to be in no condition to notice whether or not they're being remembered, I count and name the dead because—unreasonably, insistently, incorrigibly—I continue to believe they know I do.

What Else I Remember

I'm glad I remember the people I've loved and lost.

I wish I took pride in the other things I recall.

But Liz Taylor had seven husbands,

And Snow White had seven dwarfs,

And I am ashamed to admit I can name them all.

For on matters too insignificant to mention

My brain insists on maintaining total retention.

My Social Security number? I don't know it.

But I still can explain the lyrics of "Mairzy Doats."

I can do ya that ad for Brylcreem

And for J-E-L-L-O,

But I'd rather be doing Proust and Joyce Carol Oates,

Or quoting quotes from the Platos and Socrateses.

But my brain continues doing what it damn pleases.

I believe there is limited room inside my head,

And it seems to be overflowing with silly stuff.

I can't critique cryptocurrency,

Or analyze AI,

But if you should ask I can tell you more than enough

About hubba-hubba; and Jack, Doc, and Reggie;

The Edsel; and Betty Boop; and I'm wondering why,

When I'd hoped to be one of those intellectual whizzes,

I've turned into someone who knows who each husband of
    Liz is.

Note: For a little more information on Liz Taylor's seven husbands, etc.,
see the Endnotes.

Note: I still can't manage to memorize my Social Security number, so I'm
planning to be buried with it instead, just in case there's an Afterward—a
place you go after you're dead—but they won't let you in till you've filled
out all the paperwork.

Afterward

I now have reached that age when there's no such thing as hypochondria, when any lump, bump, bruise, or cough could mean fatal, when the test I'm taking tomorrow or the scan I had last week might bring me definitive news that the end is near. So I'm giving a lot more thought, though I have always given a lot of thought, to mortality—to what will happen Afterward, when we go from going to gone, from present to passed, to what will happen after we are dead.

I've also given some thought, and talked with others who've given some thought, about how, after death, we'd like to be remembered. What do we most want recognized in our obituary? What qualities do we hope will leap to mind? What are we the proudest of? What do we aspire to be our legacy? What do we want inscribed—not just on our tombstone, but in the hearts of those we've left behind?

Actually, there are several things I'd very much like to be remembered for, and I wrote about them a few years back in a poem that I aspirationally called "My Legacy."

Since it's looking as if my legacy isn't shaping up to be
Peace on earth and universal health care,
Here's what I'm hoping to be remembered for:

Showing up when I say I'm showing up.
Sticking with what I've started until it's done.
Sending valentines to all the children in our family (until
they reach the age of twenty-one).
And never, ever leaving the house without eyeliner.

Playing a relentless game of Scrabble.
Keeping the secrets I promised I would keep.
Being able to laugh about the bad things that happen to me
(Though not before I first whine, and weep, and rail
against my fate, and blame my husband).

Doing work I'm able to be proud of.
Making a truly transcendent matzoh ball.
Coming to terms with mortality (though, to be perfectly
honest,
I'm still not feeling all that thrilled about dying).

Coming to terms with not feeling thrilled about dying.

Watching over the people that I love.
(Grateful they're watching over me as well.)
Enjoying whatever there is to enjoy until that final,
time's-up, closing bell.
And hoping—just a reminder—that I'll be remembered.

I have to confess, however, that if I were only allowed one word to describe what I most value about myself, what leaps to mind is always a workaday, boring, almost embarrassing word: RELIABLE. That's right—reliable. I always do what I promise I'll do—not perfectly, but the best I can do, and I always do it on time, and I'm on time too. I've never been late for a deadline or date except for one fateful spring in the 1970s, when Robby Altman missed his second grade's fifty-yard dash on Field Day because I, the carpool driver that day, got confused about when the race was supposed to begin, and arrived—to my horror—after it was over. That happened about fifty years ago. I haven't been late since then. But I've never forgiven myself—and neither has Robby.

On the other hand, if I had *two* words to describe my proudest achievement, those words would unquestionably be MY SONS, whose praises I'll try to refrain from singing here. My father once said of my children that "they're the best books you ever wrote," and I unhesitatingly agree with him.

Marna, a hugely successful lawyer—once profiled as the Diva of Divorce, and first woman president of the D.C. Bar— immediately replied when asked to name her proudest achievement, "my son and my daughter," describing with enormous pride not their impressive CVs but their courage and decency. And Naomi, a child and adolescent developmental consultant, said, "I'm proud of having given my best to every patient I saw. I'm proud of my lengthy friendships and of being there for my friends in good times and bad. But I'm proudest of all of the daughters I raised—proud of the smart, warm, kind, engaging, liberal, generous people they have become."

Naomi and Marna were typical of *almost* every one of the many accomplished women (all mothers) I spoke with, who, when I posed the question "What are you proudest of?" answered in an identical way: My children. My children. My children. The men and women my sons and daughters are today. And while all of these women also took enormous pride in their work in government, mental health, the law, the arts, they showed no reticence saying that their children—just like mine—were indeed the best books they ever wrote.

Lucinda was the "almost" I mentioned in the preceding paragraph. Here's what she said:

"Proudest of? Most women would say their children. But not me. Proud would imply I was happy with the way I raised them. Being the perfectionist that I am, I am not impressed that I didn't meet my Donna Reed standard."

(Note: Donna Reed, star of the popular fifties–sixties family sitcom *The Donna Reed Show*, played, explains Lucinda, "a loving, smiling, calm, benign mother, capable of taking care of everything." Lucinda decided, when she was young, that she would be that kind of mom. She wasn't. Who was?)

So while she is proud of a wide range of her achievements, from fighting back against a sadistic boss, to her civic volunteering, to her art, she says she can't take credit for, although she's deeply grateful for, her "accomplished, loving, fun, funny, smart, tolerant, inquisitive, compassionate" daughters.

When I talked to men about their proudest achievement, their children were never once the first to be named, though all the dads, after a while, added that—certainly! of course!—they took pride in their kids. But here are their first responses:

George, who at ninety-nine deservedly revels and takes pleasure in his clearly still alert and questing mind, said that he'd like his tombstone, if he has a tombstone, to read: "He asked good questions." Dick hopes to be remembered for a glorious professional achievement: having been named, by a top trade publication, as the creator of one of the "best major marketing campaigns of the twentieth century." And Howard is most proud, he says, of the way he has lived his life. For though, he concedes, "there is stuff that I'd change, stuff that I'd do better, stuff I'd rewind if I could rewind the tape," he feels that he's been basically decent, honest both "with others and with myself," and "responsible both personally and socially."

He aspires, in other words, to be remembered as a "mensch," and if that's how people do remember him when he's gone, "I will come back, and kiss them on both cheeks."

Folks were extremely gracious when, soon after I said hello, I'd remind them of their mortality and ask them how they'd like to be remembered. Most of them were willing to give the matter some serious thought, and even willing to offer an opinion on what happens to us after we are dead.

But before I get to that I think I should mention, right around now, that I'm what might be called obsessed with nonexistence. My first thought, every morning, upon awakening, is that I'm going to die—and pretty soon. This is not an irrational notion, though I'm in (Knock wood! Knock wood!) excellent health—given the fact that I'm ninety-four years old, which means that in six more years I'll be one hundred. I'd say that thoughts of mortality—and what comes after death—are perfectly appropriate at my age.

But awareness of our mortality can swamp us, at any age, with fear of death, with existential dread. And so, says a theory, mincing no words, that psychologists call "terror management," we may defend ourself against the awareness that we will die someday by subscribing to some system of belief which offers us a view of the world that is larger and more enduring than that of one terrified, terminal human being. Which offers us, after our physical bodies are gone, some meaningful alternate vision of immortality.

I've written a lot about death—the death of others as well as my own, presenting consoling theories about varieties of post-mortem continuity: through our children, our art, our good works, our oneness with nature, through assorted other connections and contributions that link us with something larger than ourself, and through various scenarios—some literal, some far more abstract—of an actual death-transcending Afterlife. I've also brooded, plenty, often in verse, about how scary the prospect of being dead can be and what a terrible sport I am about it, described here in a poem I unabashedly titled "On Not Being a Good Sport About the Fact That I'm Going to Die One of These Days."

Unlike the seasons, no springtime will follow my winter.
Unlike a clock, my twelve midnight won't tick-tock
toward one.
The wind's at my back and it's turning me into a sprinter,
Rushing along on a journey that's soon to be done.

Unlike a book, I can't start again from the beginning.
Unlike a video movie, I cannot rewind.
The ice that is under my feet keeps on thinning and thinning.
Do I mind? Do I *mind?* You bet your sweet ass I mind.

My younger sister, Lois, who died of cancer at age fifty, managed to achieve a much better attitude, fighting fiercely until her last breath to survive, while all the time maintaining a remarkably calm acceptance of her death. "I wasn't around for millions and millions of years before I was born," she used to tell me. "So I don't expect to be bothered when I'm also not around for millions and millions of years after I'm dead."

I greatly admired her attitude but later wrote a poem called "Mortal Question," exploring why it didn't work for me.

I did not know I wasn't there.
I will not know I'm not.
Between these two oblivions
My life unfolds its plot.

I missed the glory that was Greece.
I missed Rome's rise and fall.
My absence from these grand events
Disturbed me not at all.

Nor did I feel deprived because
They held the Renaissance
Some centuries before my birth.
No pre-existence wants

Imposed themselves upon my peace.
Why does some future spring
Collapse my heart with longing when
I will not feel a thing?

In other words, I didn't know what I'd missed before I was born, until I was born. I now know what is there to be missed when I'm dead. But it doesn't seem to cheer me that in death I will no longer know or feel anything. Though I can't miss it then—when I'm dead—I miss it right now.

The poet Philip Larkin has described death as a state of senselessness—no taste, no touch, no smell, no sight, no sound, with "nothing to think with" and "nothing to love or link with." And though my sister seemed to find solace in a vision of absolute and eternal oblivion, Larkin clearly did not. And neither do I.

Nor can I be helped by the consolations mentioned earlier—by descendants, achievements, a oneness with the world. As for living forever in any kind of Afterlife, I find that almost impossible to imagine. Which is why I started asking people in their Final Fifth if they had some fairly specific and comforting vision of living after they were dead.

Almost all of the people I asked—which will probably tell you what kind of folks I hang out with—immediately replied, "When you're dead, you're dead." Some said "no" but ruefully added some version of, "But I really wish I did." Others said "no" but offered to elaborate on what an ideal Afterlife should be.

Gina said that sometimes she didn't and sometimes she did believe, still in some way attracted to the simple religious imagery of her childhood, "with its angels and haloes and wings and harps and everyone singing in a heavenly chorus. And I would hate it!"

Among those imagining an ideal Afterlife for themselves or for someone they loved was a husband fondly visualizing his amateur painter wife receiving daily painting lessons from Rembrandt, and a wife who pictured her ardently chess-playing husband playing each day with the chess champs of the world, and Sally proposing an intergalactic book club. And more than one person I talked with hoped that life after death could be an eternal graduate school, where he or she would have sufficient time to finally learn "everything about everything."

My beautiful friend Carolyn was the only one of my close friends who expressed a profound conviction that there was an Afterlife, but said "the where and the how and the what to do are all very secondary to my personal relationship with God." She had fallen in love with God as a child, and had lived out a love relationship that felt mutual but—down here on earth— incomplete. And though, she says, "there's a little bit of heaven here and now," it can't compare to the "uninterrupted, unadul- terated communion" that she believes awaits her in the Afterlife.

Carolyn lives in this world. She has children and grandchil- dren, friends and relatives, and some work. She's in no hurry to check out life after death. But loving God, as Scripture has told her to do, "with all your heart, with all your mind, and with all your strength," she is ready to spend eternity enjoying "a mu- tuality taken to its ultimate dimension."

In a similar vein I talked with a lively and interesting woman named Page, a ninety-seven-year-old Presbyterian widow who lives contentedly in our RC and who comfortably and clearly believes in an Afterlife. Like Carolyn's, Page's After- life offers no concrete visions of heavenly mansions or celestial activities—"that's nothing," she says, "that we could possibly know." But she deeply believes in grace, and that as a recipient of God's grace, she will spend eternity "in the arms of God."

Page urged me to read Denise Levertov's brief, exquisite poem "The Avowal," which precisely, she told me, mirrored her own beliefs, with its faith in an effortless grace and its se- rene trust in the "deep embrace" of the Creator. Thanks to her faith, Page finds that she is not afraid of death—"I just don't want dying," she says, "to take too long." And while she isn't sure whether or not she'll meet family members when she dies, she did say a tender "yes" to her dying husband when he wistfully inquired, "Will you come find me?"

Pru, on the cusp of eighty, has a dramatically different vision of life after death, telling me that "if you believe in Christ—which I do—you believe in rebirth," and that the rebirth she believes in is reincarnation.

"I believe we get to start over again and live a whole different life, a life which will allow us to try to resolve the problems and conflicts we left behind. It's a second chance to fix the things we've done, things that hurt ourself and that hurt others."

Pru hopes that reincarnation will also offer her—one of these lifetimes—a chance to fulfill her dream of exploring space. As a lover of science fiction, especially *Star Trek*, "I know," she says, "there's life out there, and I would like to see what's going on!" And while she offered no theories as to who will decide upon her next incarnation, or the qualifications for a good assignment, a life of intergalactic exploration is certainly "something I would look forward to."

A variety of visions of what an Afterlife might be like can be found in books, plays, movies, and other outlets, including a charming, irreverent TikTok series which features Denise, Heaven's gum-chewing receptionist. Denise decides who has earned some heavenly points by doing good, or lost points because of intolerance, greed, or unkindness, denying a mom who'd rejected her gay son an upgrade to an Angel Premium Plus. Liberals possessing a sense of humor don't have to be believers to appreciate a Heaven which has room for unwed mothers and a salad bar.

For a vision of an Afterlife that includes the downside— Hell—we can take a look at Dante's fearsome *Inferno*, where transgressions are eternally and garishly punished by: Being sunk in a boiling sea of blood. Being completely submerged in a lake of ice. Being gnawed on, over and over, by Harpies. Among other equally unattractive options.

I've been told of people who choose to close their minds to belief in an Afterlife because they're worried they'll wind up in Hell, not Heaven.

One of my favorite answers to my questions about an After-life was a parable that was offered in *Your Sacred Self*, a book by Dr. Wayne Dyer. In this clever tale two babies living in their mother's womb—call them Baby A and Baby B—are arguing whether there's life after delivery. Baby A considers the notion nonsense. How would they walk? How would they eat? What kind of life could such a life possibly be? Baby B insists that maybe they'll walk and eat and live in ways that they simply can't imagine right now, that maybe they'll have legs to walk on, that they might not need an umbilical cord anymore, that perhaps there'll even be a little more light. The argument continues, with Baby A shrewdly pointing out that no one has ever returned from After Delivery and that therefore After Delivery "is nothing but darkness and silence and oblivion." But Baby B is unconvinced; he insists that after delivery they will meet Mother and Mother will take care of them, a statement that Baby A finds utterly laughable. Because if Mother existed, he points out to Baby B, how can it be that no one has ever seen her?

The story ends with Baby B proclaiming to Baby A that they are and have always been surrounded by Mother, and that, if they're quiet and listen carefully, "you can hear Her loving voice calling down from above." For us atheists and skeptics this tale will have too decisive a moral but I think that by making its point so engagingly, it pays proper respect to the view that whatever happens after we're dead remains and will surely always remain a mystery.

Which hasn't prevented vast numbers of us—including those who insist "when you're dead, you're dead"—from harboring hopes, opinions, beliefs, and even some helpful suggestions about an Afterlife.

An Afterlife

Although I don't believe in it,

My hopes for an Afterlife include

The everyday as well as the divine,

Which means that in addition to

Hanging out with heavenly hosts and hostesses,

Plus an assortment of other celestial beings,

I'd spend eternity with the people I love,

And never see those I could spend forever not seeing,

Particularly (please check attached list) my sister-in-law.

Although I'm not expecting it,

My plans for an Afterlife include

The frivolous as well as the profound,

Which means that in addition to

Grasping the ultimate nature of good and evil,

Plus how much of life is free will and how much is fate,

I'll be able to play the piano without taking lessons,

Eat whatever I want without gaining weight,

And get to have sex with Paul Newman without feeling
　　guilty.

Although I wouldn't count on it,

My goals for an Afterlife include

The down-to-earth as well as the sublime,

Which means that in addition to

Purging my heart of sin and my soul of envy

Plus ridding my spirit of selfishness and despair,

I'd concede that my friend Irene is better at Scrabble,

Admit that I haven't quite mastered learning to share,

And get over the fact that Fran Tepper, who—let me tell
　　you—doesn't deserve this,

Is married to someone who worships the ground she walks on.

Although I'm not disputing it,

My views of an Afterlife include

The dubious as well as the devout,

Which means that in addition to

My awe at the magnificence of creation,

I'm wondering what the creators were thinking about

When they decided, for instance, to make mosquitoes.

And weren't there any better options than death?

And why give a chronic skin disease to a darling person like
Marilyn,

and a perfect complexion to a bitch like Beth?

And why leave us never knowing,

Never ever, for sure, really knowing

If there is an Afterlife?

Happiness

Whatever will or won't happen to us in the Afterlife, we should try, while we're here, to enjoy not being dead, engaging in our inherent and inalienable human right—the pursuit of happiness. And perhaps we'll find ourself asking—as we wander and ponder our way through our Final Fifth—whether we're happy (whatever we mean by happy), and what we could do if we wished to be happier now.

What makes people happy, late in life, is of course specific to each particular person, but the fundamentals of happiness tend to include: deep and caring relationships, good health, financial security, some satisfaction and pride in what we've achieved, and the ability to appreciate, and find meaning in, whatever it is that we are doing today.

I asked a half dozen women and men, all in their fifth-fifth, what, at this time of life, and not counting their children or their grandchildren, made them happy. Ralph, who can't remember how long he's been married, rather cryptically said, "When my wife is happy, I'm happy." Arnold, without hesitation, replied, "Playing a good game of golf on a perfect spring day." Two people spoke of encounters they have with various natural wonders—a sunset, a waterfall—that soothe their spirit, chase their worries away. Mickey asked, "Who told you I was happy?" And Sonia said, "What makes me happy is doing meaningful work, which for me is writing. It gives me the sense there's good reason to still be around."

Memories of the past can also be an important source of happiness now, as the British author Diana Athill writes in her feisty memoir:

> In the course of the ninety-seven years through which I have lived I have collected many more images of beautiful places and things . . . and now it seems as though they are jostling to float into my mind . . . shouldering aside even the most passionate love affairs and the most satisfying achievements, to make a very old woman's idle days pleasant. . . .

Though you may not think that a merely pleasant day should be counted as happy, I get the feeling that lots of us old folks do, ceding high rapture, ecstasy, bliss, and roller-coaster intensity to our youth, while our "happy" tends to express itself now as peaceful, contented, satisfied, untroubled, or—upon receiving good news about that biopsy—vastly relieved.

*

It has sometimes been said that happiness is a choice that we can make, a statement with which I both do and don't agree. For we surely need to acknowledge that there are terrible things that can and sometimes do happen, can happen to you and to those we hold dear and to me, things that can't be surmounted—either on our part or on theirs—by a better attitude or a more positive response or a tougher hide. But we also have the power, even this late in our life, to actually make some happiness-helping choices, choices that lead to changes that help make life happier.

For instance, I've been noticing that it's easy when we get old to have our feelings hurt—to feel marginalized, neglected, passed over, left out. Our daughter-in-law isn't calling us to go shopping. Our grandsons prefer playing soccer to Scrabble with us. Our son and his family have rented a house at the beach—we love the beach—but they haven't invited us to come for a visit. Not even for a weekend! Even though they've rented it for a month!

Furthermore, as Roger Angell has observed, people don't seek our opinions much anymore. Or pay attention when we offer them anyway. Plus our children keep saying, "You already told us that story." Plus our grandchildren seem to often talk over our head. Add to this the ageism we feel that we too frequently encounter and, though none of this qualifies as elder abuse, it can—if we let it—seriously hurt our feelings.

I suspect that, without half trying, we in the Final Fifth of life could manage to have our feelings hurt every day.

And we could sink into self-pity, we could silently sulk in our tent, we could guilt-trip our negligent family, we could say something snarky to those uninterested friends, we could snap "I'm not your sweetie" at some hapless drugstore clerk— none of which would contribute to our happiness. Or instead we could choose to recognize that people have busy lives, that we're not necessarily anyone's top priority, that the beach house is barely big enough for their family, that we've probably told that story—though it's a really terrific story—several times, and that when we're with our grandkids we're going to feel excluded from lots of conversations, not because we're actively being dissed (are they still saying "dissed"?) but because they're talking too fast (and not loudly enough) about athletes and bands and devices and pop stars they don't take the time to explain and that we never heard of. We could choose to feel overlooked, or underestimated, or patronized, or ignored. Or choose to decide that life is too short for hurt feelings.

A more popular and incessantly recommended route to happiness is cultivating an "attitude of gratitude," ungrateful though we may feel entitled to be. There are now some recent studies citing the many benefits of counting our blessings, like enhanced self-esteem and diminished anxiety, which could, if we started counting, make us happier. And if we wanted to go all the way and keep, as recommended, a Gratitude Journal, recording for what and to whom we should feel grateful, who knows what heights of happiness we might achieve.

(Note: When I was growing up, I was surrounded by many relatives whose constant refrain was, "As long as you have your health," for they counted good health—while offering updates on everyone's current afflictions—among the very greatest of life's blessings. Back then, not knowing better, I regarded their words with scornful disrespect, astonished that their aim would be so low. Seriously—as long as you have your health? That's something to be thrilled about—good health? How limited, how boring, how absolutely pitiful is that! Now, of course, when I clink a glass with anyone near my age, our toast in every language is always "to health." Definitely not pitiful or boring. Worthy of top billing in a Gratitude Journal.)

I cannot talk about gratitude without mentioning my friend Ellie, whose embrace of all that was good in her life—loving parents, a great marriage, terrific kids and grandkids, devoted friends—kept her sunny soul sunny and helped her survive and thrive in spite of many sorrows: The premature death of her dearly beloved sister. The sudden, untimely death of her younger son. And so many caretaking duties that she hardly had time to tell her friends she had lung cancer. Nor did this Nobel laureate of gratitude have any room or patience for self-pity.

"Kick me in the head," she would say, "if you ever hear me complain. I have had a blessed life."

We might also choose to be happier by finding someone that we can guide or mentor, someone who would be glad to take what we've got. For we all, at this age, believe we have so much wisdom and life experience to impart. But are our own kids interested? Certainly not! But other children—other people's children—may actually want it, use it, thank us for it, a sweet and surprising extra helping of happiness.

What I'd very much like to suggest, as another way of promoting happiness, is trying to bring more laughter into our life, on the grounds that if happiness sometimes can make us laugh, maybe laughing can sometimes make us happy. It's good to share laughs with our family and friends. It's essential to be able to laugh at ourself. And it's great to figure out that some of the things we had once whined and wept and wailed about are, on second thought, hysterically funny. It used to take us too long to get over whatever it was we needed to get over, but we simply don't have that kind of time anymore. We should, in late life, and despite the many sorrows of the world, accelerate—not just cultivate, but accelerate—a sense of humor, a readiness to laugh.

(Note: I've noticed that people don't seem to be telling each other jokes anymore, so I'm going to offer one here to fill the gap, a joke I heard from two different sources, one of them old enough to express relief at remembering the punch line.

An elderly man tells his elderly wife he is planning to fire the pool boy. She eloquently, vociferously objects, mobilizing her arguments from an Intro to Psychology course she's taking. "Your problem," she explains to him, "is that you've gotten old, and the presence of this attractive, zesty, hard-bodied, vital young man is a painful reminder of your mortality. You're obviously in denial about your mortality. And that's the reason why you want to fire him."

Her husband has listened patiently but now can stand no more, shaking his head in an irritated no. "That's not why I am planning to fire the pool boy," he explains to her. "I'm firing him because we don't have a pool.")

And here's some how-to-be-happier guidance that everyone ought to agree on: We need to ask for help when we need help. Help when we're going up and down steep stairs. Or carrying heavy bags from the grocery store. Or reaching for a bowl on a too-high shelf. There are things we once did that we simply can't do anymore, which means that if we climb up that ladder we're sure to wind up on the floor, to be followed by a couple of months of rehab. Embarrassing though it may feel to ask for assistance, it feels even worse to wear a hospital gown. So if we in the Final Fifth wish to be happier, or happy, or merely not miserable, we must choose as our guiding principle DON'T FALL DOWN. And the more help we get, the less likely that we'll fall down.

Though I'm deeply committed to being cautious and asking for help and never falling down, I must acknowledge that for some folks in late life—not a lot, but some—happiness includes a measure of daring, a satisfaction of their need for adventure.

As a result there are people over eighty, over ninety, over a hundred who engage in the not-for-sissies sport of skydiving. Which involves jumping out of a plane—sometimes accompanied, sometimes solo—to experience the thrill of falling-flying-floating down to earth, with a bird's-eye view of the beauties of the world. The older George Bush—for his seventy-fifth and his eighty-fifth and his ninetieth birthday—did it. Members of the Jumpers Over Eighty Society (JOES) have also done it. So, according to Google, has a woman from Chicago—at the staggering age of 104. I'm glad it made them happy. I'm not doing it.

Like skydiving, there's no such thing as too old to join the Peace Corps, which is how Alice Carter, age eighty-seven, became the Peace Corps' oldest volunteer. A lifelong social activist, she lived in many places, raised six children, and was tutoring inner-city kids in Boston when, having learned that her age was not prohibitive, she signed up for Peace Corps service in Morocco. "I'm not here to be a world-beater or accomplish impossible tasks," she once explained, adding—perhaps to encourage us to be bolder—that when you're old "you can have a really good time in the Peace Corps."

Though I didn't know Alice Carter or President Bush, I do know Patsy, an adventurer like no one I've ever met, a woman who, at eighty-two, has been to eighteen more countries than there are years in her life.

The Virginia that Patsy was raised in was affluent, rigid, full of rules and expectations, "with many social issues, many racial issues," resulting in what she called "a frozen life." But everything started to change when she spent her junior year of college in India, encountering new people and new possibilities. "I was searching for aliveness," she said, and India gave her a glimpse of ways of "breaking into becoming alive."

Over the years the hundred countries she's visited have offered her, she says, two invaluable gifts: Nourishing a boundless curiosity. And giving her what she describes as a wake-up call, a not-unfriendly "slap on the face," that invites her to pay close and respectful eyes-wide-open attention to the different kinds of people and the different kinds of lives that she encounters.

She has traveled with a companion, with tour groups, and sometimes on her own, though she always has someone to visit in Egypt or India or wherever her journeys take her. And while her choices of where to travel are usually pretty sensible, she has had a few, though never life-threatening, dramas:

"There were things going on in Baghdad and Afghanistan while I was there. And something with Hezbollah in southern Lebanon. And when I was in Syria, it happened to be in the middle of a war." These events, though sobering, have not made Patsy significantly more cautious, or less adventurous.

She will, however, because her next trip—to the Baltics—calls for two to five miles of walking each day, defer to her age by skipping a few expeditions. But she knows she'll return from her travels not only filled with the wonders she's seen, but "as always, more awake to my own country." And her vital, adventurous life will keep making her feel—like the title of Diana Athill's memoir—alive, alive oh!

Shrugging off hurt feelings, cultivating gratitude, mentoring and laughing and asking for help are, along with (for some) pursuing adventure, among the ways we can choose to be happy, or happier.

And then there's the Happiness Curve.

In contrast with, or maybe in addition to, the you-can-choose-to-be-happy theory, there's this strange phenomenon called the Happiness Curve. It brings good news to us in the Final Fifth.

Much has been written about the Happiness Curve. Much

research has been assembled to prove its existence. And study after study—see *The Happiness Curve,* a book by Jonathan Rauch—leads us to the same surprising conclusion.

This U-shaped curve shows happiness to be highest in our youth, located on the upper-left side of the U, then dipping down as we head into our forties. Once we've reached the curve's bottom, we will spend some time enduring a midlife malaise (which some prefer to call a midlife crisis), after which our happiness starts climbing ever upward, making its way up the right side of the U. And continues climbing up as we grow older. And continues climbing up as we grow old.

And we are left to reckon with this strange and extremely unexpected conclusion: that after the years of our youth are over and done, we next reach the heights of happiness in—old age.

What's going on here? Why does our life hit its nadir in midlife? And why, from our late forties and fifties on, does it keep getting better?

One theory suggests that we are, in our youth, full of impossible dreams and great expectations, leaving us disappointed when, in midlife, it's becoming clear that most of them won't come true. Or perhaps we're doing okay but we insist on comparing ourselves to those who've done better, and thus keep seeing ourselves as woefully lacking. Or perhaps we're doing great—great job, great marriage, great kids, great everything—yet find ourselves, in our forties, constantly doubting and questioning our achievements. And gloomily asking ourselves, "Is that all there is?"

Having had firsthand experience with my own midlife malaise, I used to—when speaking to women's groups—complain about it, complain about the dreams (ballerina, brain surgeon, tennis star) that are, in our forties, permanently foreclosed; complain about the arrival of sagging kneecaps and laugh lines and upper-eyelid droop; complain about the bone-deep and no-longer-hypothetical realization that no matter how careful we are we someday will die. But whatever group I was talking to, and no matter what part of the country I was in, the very same thing would happen—every time. Invariably some woman in the audience would raise her hand to inform me, "Wait until your fifties—it gets so much better."

So, long before I'd ever heard of this thing called the Happiness Curve, I was—kind of, sort of—waiting for things to get better. And they did.

Here's how Rauch and other researchers explain it:

Simply by virtue of reaching our age—this fiftyish postmidlife age—we have entered a new stage of adult development, a stage, according to Rauch, where there "is a change in our values and sources of satisfaction," a change (that might be hardwired) "in *who we are*," a change that can extend—despite infirmities and fragilities—into old age. Our ambitions are tamed. Our expectations are modified. We're comparing ourself not to others but to ourselves. And we're starting to feel contented. And we're starting to feel grateful. And we're starting to feel it's a pretty good life after all.

This increase in positive feelings even seems to hold up in *very* old age because, as one researcher puts it, while old age "has its share of hardships and disappointments . . . by the time people get there they're more attuned to the sweetness of life than to its bitterness."

So what is my opinion—my personal, nonscientific opinion—about the Happiness Curve?

Four years ago, at age ninety, I was asked: If given the choice, which decade of my life would I want to return to. And I truly astonished myself when the answer that unexpectedly came to me was, "I'd just like to push the hold button down on RIGHT NOW." I then explained that I'd chosen right now because I was a very lucky lady. Lucky because I still loved, and still was married to, the man I'd been married to for sixty-one years, despite his ridiculous claim that he could read the *Times* and listen to me simultaneously. Lucky because all my children and my grandchildren, as of that moment, were doing just fine. Lucky because I had friends with whom I continued to share a deep and enduring history. Lucky because I'd somehow (again, at least as of that moment) been spared time's harsher assaults on my body and mind.

And since, in addition to lucky, I am a quite superstitious lady, I kept knocking wood as I cataloged my good fortune. But just a few weeks short of our sixty-third anniversary, my husband—my dear Milton—suddenly died. And I wasn't feeling so lucky anymore.

I've now joined many people I know in the Final Fifth of life who may previously have experienced, but no longer are experiencing, the onward and upward swing of the Happiness Curve. And what with the health and human losses that time inevitably, inexorably brings, I don't see happiness heading north indefinitely. It makes sense to me that we who can learn to love not only spring but all the seasons can find a growth in happiness even in the winter of late life. But I suspect that at some point it will stop growing.

Which doesn't mean giving up trying to be happy. And which also reminds me I've got one more thought about how:

Help save the world.

We in the Final Fifth may tell ourselves we've had a good run, and that we're getting out in the nick of time, regretful that we're leaving a terrible mess for the next generations, but figuring that we did what we could—now it's *their* turn.

And it's certainly true that we tried—we marched for peace and civil rights, we picketed and protested and petitioned, stuffed envelopes and knocked on doors and mailed out checks to many worthy causes, and housed and fed friends and strangers who kept pouring into D.C. to rally on behalf of a better world. But the world we live in today is in an even more perilous state and it's time to hand it over to those who must fix it. And we may feel a need to apologize as we make our way to the exit end of the stage. Except . . .

Except we're still here. Except we haven't left yet. Except there is work that even we old folks can do. So why not find some small something to do to help save this wounded planet? Why not find something constructive to do and—just do it?

Now, we in the Final Fifth may feel we've aged out of saving the world. Not true. For if body and mind are fairly intact, and if we've got the time, and a lot of us do, why not put ourselves out there for causes we care about? Why not explore (by contacting organizations we support) the ways in which, in addition to sending a check, we could do some small something more about matters like climate change, gun control, human rights, civil rights, choice?

We may choose to be an activist like Mary Church Terrell, who, in her eighties, back in 1950, marched in D.C. picket lines protesting segregation in theaters and restaurants. We may choose, as some of us did a few years back with a protest group called Firehouse Fridays (set up by Jane Fonda, another late-life activist), to spend some hours under arrest after decorously demonstrating against climate change. (The challenge here was not being able to pee from ten in the morning till six at night.) But even if we don't have either the stamina or the bladder for such activities, there is good stuff a person can do without leaving home.

For instance, in the months before the crucial election of 2024, a friend of mine delivered to my RC apartment door one thousand get-out-the-vote preprinted postcards. My job was to add a brief encouraging note to every card, a personal touch that might help to seal the deal, which I did by composing some earnest, upbeat, very (and I mean very) simple poems, one or another of which I inscribed on each postcard. Doing a batch of twenty a day, with mellow music playing in the background, I spent a small portion of fifty truly soul-satisfying mornings doing my small something to help save the world.

Now, there's no guarantee that anything we do can make anything better. But between our physical therapy and our trips to the cardiologist we could try. And find, in the trying, new reasons to enjoy not being dead. And find, in the trying, a little more happiness now.

Getting Out the Vote

1.

It's voting time.
I'm back in touch
To say your vote
Counts very much.

2.

Here is a message
I'm proud to promote:
Democracy needs you.
Be sure to vote.

3.

I'm writing this upside
down
To get your attention.
But getting you to vote
Is my only intention.

Loneliness

Home alone writing messages that we hope will get out the vote and perhaps save the world may indeed be gratifying, even soul satisfying. But too much time alone can leave us lonely. And despite the devices connecting us to family and friends, and strangers, all over the world, we—and that "we" includes both the young and the old—are confronting, right now, an epidemic of loneliness.

In May 2023 the surgeon general of the U.S., Dr. Vivek Murthy, issued an advisory, a serious public health warning, about the mental and physical dangers of loneliness, a condition that amazingly is afflicting some 50 percent of American adults. And while younger adults are almost twice as likely as those over sixty-five to feel lonely, many of us in our Final Fifth are dealing with various age-related realities that isolate us and limit our human connections.

We're cut off from human connections because of our aches and pains and physical limitations; or because we find ourselves needing more from others than they may be willing or able to provide; or because social isolation (we no longer drive; we've moved to a hard-to-reach location) is limiting our social participation; or because too many of those who comprised our dearest and deepest relationships have become in some way lost to us—or have died.

Leaving us feeling scared, sad, abandoned—and angry. Leaving us feeling anxious and depressed. Leaving some of us feeling profoundly ashamed, too ashamed to confess to *anyone*, how desperately hungry we are for human connection.

The death of people we love is very likely to be our greatest source of loneliness. But connections can also fray with important people in our life when the experiences we shared and the wonderful ways we were together are no longer either feasible or fun. Relationships may change or even vanish when we need to schlep our oxygen tank to the theater, or a stroke makes it hard for people to grasp what we say, or we're no longer able to join in any three-generation vacations involving bikes or hikes or merely a rental house with too tricky a walk to the beach.

Even a meal at a restaurant can feel more like work than play—discouraging to us but often more discouraging to the companion who is doing the heavy lifting. And maybe, before we fault that companion for lacking in compassion, patience, or competence, we might try to see things from his or her point of view.

I've merged many stories I've heard about taking an elderly friend or relative to a restaurant into one essentially true but composite account, with a woman I'll call Pam describing the multiple challenges of a lunch date with her ninety-plus-year-old uncle:

Get him into the car, then fold and try to jam his walker into the trunk. Help him to fasten his seat belt, which his arthritis makes it hard for him to do. Then help him to find his lost shoe, which somehow fell off while he was trying to fasten that seat belt.

Double-park at the restaurant. Wrestle the walker out. Guide him to his table and his seat. Double knot his shoelaces so the shoes will stay on his feet while you're parking the car.

Don't say something ungracious when, after a sweaty walk back from the parking garage, he asks why it took you so long to park the car.

And then, since his eyesight is bad and the restaurant lighting absurdly dim, read the menu to him so he'll know what his choices are, often repeating a reading because his hearing aids are no match for this noisy restaurant.

Order and eat. Ask the waitress to wipe up the spillage. Guide him to the men's room, making sure he won't trip on the napkin that fell off his lap. Go get the car. Get him into the car. Get him and his walker back home. Then take a deep breath. Take another deep breath. Take a nap.

Pam will go out with her uncle again (to a place with more light and less noise), and she'll do her best to do it with a smile. But this wasn't an easy enterprise and she won't be making another date for a while. And her absence will be one more absence for her uncle in a life which, through nobody's fault, is getting lonelier.

If we're in our fifth-fifth of life, chances are that our sight has declined, and our hearing has also declined, and we huff and we puff when we're climbing up stairs or a hill. And if that problem with our left leg doesn't restrict our activities, that pain in our needs-a-replacement right hip surely will. And it's awkward to go for a walk when, out of the blue, the world starts swirling around and around and we're all of a sudden in danger of losing our balance. Plus it's looking like rain, so wherever it was that we were planning to go, why don't we all just forget it and stay home?

This is how some of us older folks, constrained by various physical limitations, find ourselves excluded, or decide to exclude ourselves, decide it's safer and easier to stay home.

It can get lonely being home alone. And, as daylight fades and another empty evening descends, we may start brooding:

Why doesn't someone call to ask how we're doing? How can a whole day go by and the phone doesn't ring? How can a whole day go by and we haven't accomplished one damn thing besides making the bed and watering a few houseplants? We've lost our will, our energy, our interest in the world. We don't even know who we are without someone to see us. We want to be protected and taken care of. We want someone to take over our life and help free us from the burden of creating a life on our own.

From the burden of being so deeply, deeply alone.

From the burden of trying to make the best of what's left of it.

For some lonely people the overriding feeling is abandonment; for others it is abject helplessness. "Helpless," says Audrey, "is my middle name. I have trouble being alone because I'm scared something bad will happen and there won't be anybody here to help me." Age eighty-four and widowed, she urgently tries to fill up her days with friends to have meals with, see movies with, just hang out with, "but I don't seem to have enough friends to fill all the slots."

And she'll sometimes sound almost aggrieved (but it's her desperation talking) about the friend who's spending so much time with her grandchildren, or the friend whose husband always wants her around, or the friend who has decided to take up pickleball, or the friend who's taking another trip out of town. Friends who are otherwise occupied instead of occupied with lonely Audrey.

And when I suggest volunteer work to alleviate her loneliness, she says she's the one who needs a volunteer. Specifically what she needs is "the right person—a woman or man—to move in here with me and be my grown-up."

"I am definitely," she points out to me in case I hadn't noticed it, "too needy."

Her neediness, she sometimes fears, may be driving people away, and sad to say this very well may be true. But though she asks a lot she is funny and smart, has a loving heart, and a lot to give—if only she weren't so desperately lonely too.

In talking with Vincent, a man in his middle nineties, I was hearing about a different kind of loneliness—a loneliness for a life he had loved and lost, a life he misses every day. A retired psychologist, Vincent and his much-beloved wife, Faye, married back in the fifties, settled in Washington, and lived for many years in the same apartment, one to which they were deeply attached. These years, he says, were amazing, filled with travel, good friends, and good times, and burnished by being a part— "being very much a part"—of a caring community. Add to that a marriage he describes as "close to perfect" and it's clear why he saw his life as "truly blessed."

Faye, so Vincent makes movingly clear, was the shining center of his happiness, raising the kids while he pursued his sometimes demanding career, running the household, supportive of his work, dealing with everything from reservations and repairs to investments and taxes, and always game to go on adventures with him, whether bargain hunting at a yard sale around the corner or meeting the Dalai Lama across the globe. Easygoing and supergood at whatever she chose to do, Faye was up for everything. Till she wasn't.

It began when she couldn't manage to do the taxes anymore— the numbers confused her—and then moved to a dementia diagnosis. Next they exchanged their treasured apartment for one in Assisted Living, because she was beginning to need more care. And then, as time went by and things got worse, Faye decided she wouldn't want to live much longer in her diminished state, saying she'd rather die by VSED—voluntarily stopping eating and drinking. And Vincent not only supported his wife's decision; he insisted that when the time came he would be going along with her on this last journey, insisted the two of them would die together.

Their son and daughter, who, Vincent says, understood and respected their parents' choice, would, when that time came, travel across the country to say their goodbyes. But the grim new Covid-19 epidemic put travel and family gatherings on hold. And by the time the four of them could finally get together, Faye's mind was in a different place and she no longer remembered that she had wished to die.

She also was no longer able to be adequately cared for by Vincent and the folks at Assisted Living. At their children's insistence, Faye was transferred to a more protective environment, while a desolate Vincent remains in Assisted Living, visiting Faye every day around dinnertime. He always does most of the talking , reporting on what has happened that day, for Faye "can't carry on a real conversation." But she always smiles when she sees him, and she wears—every single day—the bracelet that was the very first gift he gave to her.

As for the future . . .

"I've got kidney disease, which could kill me before the year is out," Vincent tells me. "But I don't want to die and leave her here alone."

One afternoon Vincent took Faye, along with his son and grandson and me, on a nostalgic tour of their former apartment, pointing out as we moved from room to room what was new and what was as it had been when Vincent and Faye had been happily living there. Faye didn't speak a word but she had a smile on her face from the start to the end of our tour. And Vincent, recalling those sunlit days when they hadn't a clue as to what the future would bring, seemed to have found a brief escape from loneliness.

Though Audrey's and Vincent's are, I believe, extreme examples of loneliness, it's a state that in even its milder manifestations shouldn't be and hasn't been ignored. The harmful effects of loneliness, so dramatically highlighted recently by Murthy, have long been reported and analyzed and deplored, and the subject of serious research for many years. These potentially harmful effects include (and this list will probably add to Audrey's fears): heart disease, diabetes, arthritis, stroke, dementia, anxiety, depression. Plus a risk of premature death that is greater than being obese, or physically inactive. Plus a risk of premature death that's like smoking up to fifteen cigarettes a day. Not to mention an increased risk of suicide. And while researchers remind us that some people like and prefer to be alone, and that social isolation is not necessarily the same as loneliness, they also want to remind us that there are men and women out there who are always surrounded by people—and always lonely.

There is, indeed, an epidemic of loneliness.

Even loving relationships with our children and our grandchildren may not be enough to hold loneliness at bay. They may live far off—on the other side of the country, or even the world. But whether ten minutes or thousands of miles away, our kids are people with spouses and work and very active lives, and our grandkids are busy with school, first jobs, or finding themselves. Which means, that though they indeed may love us dearly, it's going to be hard for them to find a place for us on their crowded dance card.

And we'd rather not press them.

"We want to be a pleasure—not a duty or a burden," Vivian tells me. "We don't want to come off as needy or dependent. And I swear I work harder at trying to be interesting and fun with my kids and my grandchildren than I do with practically anyone else in my life."

Weekly phone calls, regular visits, family outings and trips and celebrations serve as familial antidotes to loneliness. I'm grateful to Tony and Michy for faithfully calling me every Sunday night from Denver; for my casual suppers with Alexander and Marla; for my evenings with Nick and Marya in New York. And I'm grateful that my grandkids, now grown and living all over the map, keep in touch too—Bryce sending thoughtful emails from San Francisco; Olivia, Isaac, and Toby popping over to see me whenever they're back in D.C. Last year, Miranda visited me for a lovely, long, chatty weekend, explaining that she'd come because "with all due respect, you're in your nineties. And as much as I'd like to fantasize otherwise, you won't be around forever. So I was seeking quality time to take in, while I can, the magic of our connection." To which I had nothing whatever to say except, "Wow!"

Benjamin and Nathaniel, having been gently nudged by their parents, each made a separate trip from New York to spend a weekend "getting to know their grandmother." During that delicious time we walked and talked and ate and watched TV, while they queried me on everything from my favorite foods (French, Japanese) and my favorite movie (*Lost Horizon*) and my favorite TV series (a tie between *A French Village* and *The Wire*) to what (if any) were my youthful drug habits.

To which I also had nothing whatever to say.

Grandkids are a great vaccine against loneliness.

I know some people, however, still in their home or at our RC, who have difficult family relationships and who rarely or ever see grandkids or family members. They all have compelling stories to tell about how they've tried and failed to bridge the gap. They all wish it had turned out differently. And while some have made their peace with this alienation, it remains for others a source of lingering loneliness.

There are also some who face difficulties because, when they moved to their final dwelling place, they moved from the people they'd known for large parts of their lifetime to where the only people they knew were their children. Where there were no old friends to eat dinner with or go to a play with or drink wine and spend time with. Where they found themselves asking more from their kids than it was—to be fair—reasonable to ask for. And where, when they didn't ask, they were lonely.

So what's to be done to help lonely folks feel less lonely? And what can lonely folks do to help themselves?

Meaningful relationships. Sustained involvement with others. Becoming a member of a caring community. In everything I read about addressing the problem of loneliness, the answer is connection. Human connection.

A dog can maybe help us feel less lonely. A cat can maybe help us feel less lonely. So can social media, though not everyone agrees, and only if it isn't overdone. But from knitting groups to exercise classes to pizza nights with family or walks with friends, people need people to see, be seen by, connect with. And if they can't actually meet in person, they can try to sustain connection through regularly scheduled face time and Zoom and family chats and leisurely one-on-one phone dates.

"Monthly, weekly, daily, hearing from people," says Dolores, "means that I matter, means I'm on someone's mind."

But there's nothing like actual flesh-and-blood human connections.

Great Britain, where they've creatively responded to the problem of loneliness by establishing a Ministry of Loneliness, offers examples of forging human connections. Like serving a weekly lunch at a neighborhood center so people will "get out of the house and make friends." Like arranging for get-together events like sing-alongs and Glamour Clubs (where folks are encouraged to wear their most glamorous clothing). Like "Loneliness Awareness Week," which features a range of events from poetry readings to picking up the trash. Like "The Big Help-Out" day, when, invited to come together to volunteer, six million did.

Encouraging volunteer work is a valuable way to get lonely people to help themselves. Because volunteering tends to involve connecting with other people. And because this involvement sometimes distracts from the self-involvement loneliness can generate. But helping the lonely help themselves may also require a kind but firm reminder that loneliness isn't a destiny, it's a choice, and that—like it or not, ready or not, in the mood or not—lonely people should force themselves to connect. Calling it "the medicine hiding in plain sight," Murthy explains: "It could be spending fifteen minutes each day to reach out to people we care about, introducing ourself to our neighbors, . . . sitting down with people with different views to get to know and understand them, and seeking opportunities to serve others, recognizing that helping people is one of the most powerful antidotes to loneliness."

There are songs and poems about loneliness, exhaustive studies of loneliness, a Ministry of Loneliness, an epidemic of loneliness, but some folks don't have the temperament to be lonely. I'm thinking of Irwin, age ninety-five, a longtime widower and practically blind, who never complains about loneliness and says of himself, "I think I do pretty well."

Irwin shares a house with one of his sons, and his son's family, his small but sufficient basement apartment separated from them by a stairway and door—"a DMZ between two lives." And I find it a measure of his remarkably upbeat disposition that he tells me "I've got everything I need" and insists "it's a *garden*, not a *basement*, apartment."

Irwin can't drive, he can barely read, it's too hard to watch

TV, so he lives without one. He's also the only email-less person I know. But he seems to enjoy his life, getting to where he wants to go by cab, bus, or Metro, and finding companions to go with to concerts and shows, and exploring a late-life gift for writing poetry, and "seeing as many people as I can handle," and maintaining with his son's family affectionate ties and an easy respect for each other's privacy. There are also audiobooks, and radio news, and assorted magnifying devices to help him see what is difficult to see. And, on occasion, he walks the family dog. And sometimes he goes to a neighbor's house for tea.

When I asked him what he wished he had that was lacking in his life, his first answer was his wife, the second good vision.

Irwin's near blindness, his limited funds, his basement apartment, his widowerhood could have led to isolation and loneliness. But it seems that he feels neither isolated nor lonely. During these long years without his wife, and much as he enjoys women, "I have never," he insists, "wanted another wife or companion or partner or nursemaid or caretaker." This isn't to say he'd never been up for a loving, romantic relationship. But nothing, it seems, resembling till death do us part. Why?

Because, he replied, he would not want to be a burden. Because another woman would surely compare unfavorably to his lost wife. Or maybe, as his words toward the end of our talk suggested to me, because, in a way, his wife is somehow still with him.

"I've got her picture on my fridge. I greet her in the morning. I always say good night to her at night. And sometimes I ask her advice. And sometimes I will get a little guidance."

Over the phone I can clearly hear the smile in Irwin's voice. He doesn't sound lonely.

Milton had me for companionship (along with steadfast Irwin and steadfast Mike), but I certainly couldn't replace all the friends and activities that, due to his body's impairments, were slipping away. He never complained about loneliness, though I often felt lonely *for* him, and his answer to how are you doing was always "Okay." And when it came to his family—his sons, his daughters-in-law, and his grandkids—he always tried really hard to stay in the game. And sometimes he did. And sometimes fate intervened.

Milton died before four of our grandchildren—all in the same season—were graduating from high school, grad school, and college, mostly at challenging-to-get-to locations. Constrained though he was, he'd already announced that he was intending to go to Bryce's and Miranda's and to Isaac's and Olivia's graduations, in spite of the demands of cross-country travel, multiple airports, and hostile terrain. And strenuous though this would be both for him and the family, we didn't even try to talk him out of it.

Difficult? Even perilous? Possibly impossible? Milton didn't worry, and didn't care. He wasn't going to miss these momentous events just because staying home was safer and easier. It took his death to stop him from being there.

He missed the graduations. I missed Milton.

Most of the widowed I know, including some long-standing widows and widowers, have times when they especially miss— when they are especially lonely for—their lost spouse.

For Cheryl it's after dinner "when we used to talk or quietly read our books together, and I now fill that time watching filler on TV."

For June it's over breakfast "when I miss that journalist mind of his analyzing some court decision or Yemen."

For Cole it's a radio program—playing those tunes that he and his wife had loved listening to—which, since her death, "always brings tears to my eyes."

For Viv it's at a party "that I'm going to alone and I don't know many people and no one's talking to me, and my husband isn't there for me to stand next to."

And for many of us it's waking at night and reaching our hand out to touch that familiar body—and finding we're touching the empty side of the bed.

The intensity and frequency of our widow or widower loneliness will in some measure diminish over time. Life barges in, compelling the healing to start. We'll need our human connections—our family and friends and our caring community—to be there with us and for us when loss makes us lonely. And we'll need to help ourselves, which is why I go to my desk every morning and try to write the loneliness out of my heart.

A Jewish Widow's Country-Western Love Song

I've got a home but no one to come home to.

I've got a king-size bed without a king.

Got property and money but nobody to call honey.

It only *looks* like I've got everything.

It's winter here—it only looks like spring.

I've got two tickets but one seat is empty.

Two whiskey sours—guess I'll drink the spare.

A lot of reservations to a lot of destinations

At none none none of which will he be there.

I'm always hoping but he's never there.

I just am not cut out to be a widow.

Take off my wedding ring? That's like a lie.

I used to be a missus

Kissing back my husband's kisses,

And that's who I wanna be until I die.

That's who I'm gonna be until I die.

Community

The solution to being lonely, we're told, is becoming an active part of a caring community. What lonely folks seem to need above all are continuing connections with other "living, breathing human beings." But lonely or not, and ready or not, we suddenly find ourself thrust into a community when we move from our private home to the Independent Living section of this RC. And are issued a fob to open the door to our building and our apartment; a parking space, storage unit, mailbox key; and a plastic alarm which we're supposed to hang from our neck or wrap around our wrist so that we can press it for help in case of emergency.

Along with our alarm we're given many sheets of contact information to help us reach the residents and management and staff of our friendly RC. For we are indeed known to be a friendly RC. Which—it turns out—not everybody loves. Let me tell you a story:

A few years ago a prospective resident, Rick, checked out our RC, and came away impressed with its great location, its handsome apartments, and in-house facilities. But once he got home he informed his wife, who had sent him to reconnoiter, that he couldn't possibly live there. Never! No way! Because, as he'd toured the RC, he kept meeting people who smiled and greeted him with some version of, "Hi. How are you? Have a nice day." Obliging him, he complained, to respond in turn to each one of these smiling friendly strangers. And persuading him that a move to our RC might overwhelm him with far too much community.

In contrast to this—what shall I call it?—curmudgeonly response (though I kind of get it), here's George's take on our community:

When George, with his wife, Evelyn, moved into the RC about four years ago, it felt, he said, like moving to a new planet. A neighbor of mine in Cleveland Park, he too gave up the house he had lived in for decades for apartment living among a population of women and men who, as he bluntly put it, "were all here to die."

Right now, however, George—who'll be one hundred on his next birthday—seems to be too busy to find time to die. And though he admits to having had a "very tough time" leaving his lovely old home—for reasons he wouldn't discuss because "they're personal"—one session with a therapist and "I got over it." And despite his no-nonsense we're "all here to die" perspective, he chooses to define himself as being in his NEXT, not his LAST, stage of life.

Articulate and alert and very comfortably in command of the conversation, George enthuses about this next stage of his life, happily settled in this "protective" and "very nice community," where he feels so well taken care of and "where everyone seems to get along with everyone." And while he's had some problems with his teeth, and remembering names, plus issues with stability "because my legs are getting a little cranky on me," he's a man who has clearly made this new planet his own.

He has acquired many new friends because "the people here are so friendly and easy to like." He has joined a nonfiction book group, he's taking a drawing class, and, as a member of the Food and Dining Committee, he's doing his best to upgrade the chicken breast. (FYI: Bone in, skin on, and do *not* overcook it.) He is also part of a six-person men's group—their time together "the most enjoyable part of my week," with the conversation ranging from physics to politics to food, but rarely into women, sports, or the personal.

In November 2022 George was awarded France's distinguished Légion d'honneur, presented by President Emmanuel Macron himself, to acknowledge his service to France during World War II. And though he didn't especially feel he deserved it, the experience was something of a thrill. He also bought a new car—oh, yes, he's still driving, And he also wants to understand more about physics. And he hopes to be doing something about those cranky legs of his so he can get back to playing golf with his golf buddy.

Enjoying his wife's companionship, and the attentions of his kids, and his involvement with a satisfying community, George, now hurrying off to a three o'clock meeting at the RC, is a clearly contented inhabitant of his next—not his last, but simply his next—phase of life.

Although many of us who are living here in Independent Living would probably call this the "last" phase of our life; and although one of the residents has—but not for attribution—named it "Death's Waiting Room"; and although, as George points out, we're "all here to die," the emphasis of the management and what seems like a majority of the residents is not on slowly subsiding into the sunset, but primarily, even insistently, on engagement.

Engagement in the activities, opportunities, connectivities available to us in our RC.

For a person could be busy from the lavish Sunday brunch to the weekly movie shown every Saturday night, occupying the days in between (and these are only a sampling) with committees to serve on (landscape, wellness, budget); exercise classes (aerobics, weight training, yoga); musical performances (Basie to Bach); guest lectures (about politics, science, art); and bused outings (to monuments, gardens, museums, and shopping). There are also discussion groups (current events, fiction, nonfiction). And support groups (spouses as caretakers, low-vision challenges). And game-playing groups (poker, mah-jongg, bridge). And groups with whom to speak only French, or to sing with.

Some of these activities are provided by RC management, many others begun and run by the residents, offering plenty and varied ways to pursue individual interests while collectively fostering a sense of community.

Belonging to a community means feeling or being linked to one another by something that seems to serve as connective tissue. Connected by ethnicity, nationality, heredity, or geography. By shared values, objectives, interests, ideologies. Or by all kinds of other linkages (fill in yours right here), including the many shared cycle-of-life experiences, bodily changes, and cultural references common to those of us in our Final Fifth.

Community engagement, which is ardently promoted at our RC, means that management and residents are actively working together to create a sense of inclusiveness and well-being. And while management, not the residents, runs the RC, we residents, through our committees and other avenues for expressing ourselves, are never going to lack an opportunity to communicate whatever is on our mind.

I would say that communication—I might even say *exhaustive* communication—among and between the oh-so-articulate residents and management of our RC is essential to the fostering of community.

And sometimes it's not just exhaustive—it is exhausting!

Messages telling us what's going on and what we need to know sometimes arrive in our cubbyhole, and on certain occasions over our PA system or under our door, while the TV monitors hung in our corridors offer more information and—on the right date—wish each one of us a HAPPY BIRTHDAY. There are also little desks—I call them the "death desks"—discreetly scattered in some of our public spaces, displaying photos, obituaries, and helpful information about upcoming services for the recently dead.

And that's just for starters.

Messages from the management keep popping up on our computer screen, with good news (a Beatles party, dress accordingly) and bad news (two cases of Covid in Building Nine); and reports on successful repairs (the garage door is working) or impending maintenance problems (expect excessive noise tomorrow in Building Four).

And then there's our lively residents' Listserv with information to offer on practically everything:

Recommendations of articles to read and shows to see and sights to admire and specialists to go to. Notifications of objects lost or found or that someone needs or is giving away. Kudos for special efforts and special events—we're extremely generous with our kudos. And warnings, concerns, complaints, and constructive criticism about the state of affairs at our RC.

About the food. About a mysterious substance that is causing some residents to "itchy-itch." About the food. About an anonymous dog who is relieving himself in unauthorized locations. About the food. About some weary-looking furnishings which need to be—and are currently being—upgraded so they won't make a bad impression on our visitors. About not only the food but about the typos on the menus describing the food. Flowerless chocolate cake? Honey-glazed chicken tights? Isn't anyone editing this stuff?

(Note: One of my favorite food critiques, sent directly to me by Judy S, had this to say about a dining room specialty: "Last night's Mahi-Mahi, phooey-phooey." Didn't I tell you that we're an articulate bunch?)

And we're also a very community-minded bunch.

For when it comes to strengthening the bonds of our community, some of our residents go to remarkable lengths.

Ted and his wife, Tracy, produce, and they've done this annually for eleven years, hundreds of servings of fabulous homemade soup—three different kinds!—that we're all invited to show up and enjoy. There are only two requirements, both of which are intended to foster connection. The first requirement is "Wear your name tag." The second is "CIRCULATE!"

Dan is the saintly resident who graciously volunteers to repair our computers, showing up on those desperate days when all we are able to do is tear out our hair. We in the Final Fifth, who aren't exactly on the cutting edge of technology, are deeply grateful to Dan for always, calmly and kindly, being there—to rescue both our machine, and us, from a breakdown.

And then there's Mary, who helps whenever there's something in need of help, teaching an exercise class that's lacking a teacher, or visiting with—accompanied by her homemade chocolate-chip cookies—the dwellers of Memory Care, or training a cadre of residents to man the Building Eight desk when no one is there, or—with Dan and others—organizing an in-house New Year's Eve party where everyone is welcome and there's no shame in falling asleep well before midnight.

There are all kinds of other special efforts by individuals, and by management too, to make residents—both old and new—feel welcome. But despite a lot of community outreach not everyone who comes here will find it all that easy to find their place.

Stewart, a psychiatrist who lives in our RC, offers some gentle guidance to recent residents:

"Whatever feelings you have, do not judge yourself harshly. They are the normal feelings of a sudden, or not so sudden, change of identity." This change of identity, Stewart explains, often involves your health—or your spouse's health, resulting in major changes in how you live and what you can do, and sometimes requiring you to take on new and demanding roles and responsibilities.

"These changes may make you feel you've lost the person you used to be. But new friendships and new experiences and maybe—at some point—a new buddy or a new partner, someone to love, will help to fix what needs to be repaired." Affiliation helps, he reassures us. "Affiliation tends to heal the loss."

Affiliation, however, requires some effort, some exposure. It means taking a risk by asking someone if they'd like to join you for dinner, or if there's room for you in the mah-jongg game. Some hesitate to do this because "I'm afraid of being rejected." Others say, "I'm afraid of seeming pushy." And one woman, noting the residents' often quite impressive CVs, says she hesitates to reach out, "because I'm afraid that they won't find me interesting."

On the other hand, there's Judy S, who finds the RC so interesting and so welcoming "that I've made an entirely new life for myself in old age." Having never lived, or even contemplated living, in a community, "I didn't think I could possibly fit in." Yet here she is, enjoying new friends and amiable acquaintances, and feeling "very comfortable and cozy." And, she adds, "feeling very happy and very proud of myself that I've been able to do this in my last days."

It seems to me that most of the people independently living here are feeling sufficiently comfortable and sufficiently engaged with friends and activities. It seems to me that our many shared commonalities of old age, our shared history of a pre-Beatles, pre-internet world, and our shared ineptitude with the bewildering demands of the twenty-first century are part of what connects us to each other. Above all else it seems to me, as I've talked with, and lived among, the women and the men of our RC, that we've come to like and admire and learn from and laugh with one another to a degree we could not have imagined possible, connected as a community of former strangers and now some new best friends who are doing our best with what's left in our Final Fifth.

Princess Margaret, Pearl Harbor, "Daffodils," Etc.

Though we're—most of us—short of breath and long in
   the tooth,

Though there isn't much space between our waist and
   brassiere,

Though there's been some significant shrinkage since our
   youth,

Our shared decline makes it easier living here.

Though the twenty-first century is a heavy lift,

We somehow are comforted spending time with those

Who may never have heard a song sung by Taylor Swift,

But know Princess Margaret's middle name was Rose,

And remember Pearl Harbor, if not what they just ate,

And can even recite some of "Daffodils" by heart.

Who admire our grandchildren photos: "Gorgeous!"
   "Great!"

"Looks like Grace Kelly!" "Looks like Clark Gable!"
   "Looks . . . smart!"

We're not expected to upload or even to text.

We're becoming less of an "I" and more of a "we."

And though we are surely aware of what's coming next,

We're often too busy to ponder eternity,

And glad to be in the company of those

Who know Princess Margaret's middle name was Rose.

Wisdom

The best time to plant a tree was twenty years ago.
The next-best time to plant a tree is now.

—Ancient Chinese proverb

Remembering Pearl Harbor or Princess Margaret's middle name may make for cozy communal connections but isn't likely to qualify as wisdom. Nor, says a study I recently read, do researchers agree on a correlation between wisdom and old age. However, this study also concludes that "certain life experiences tend to be wisdom producing, thus giving older people a slight advantage." So with this "slight advantage" in mind I decided to start my wisdom collecting by asking the residents of our RC, along with others in their Final Fifth, to send me some piece of advice, some helpful thoughts on the nature of life and how best to live it, that they think could be useful to younger generations, or that they find useful in their own life right now.

Many of the replies I received emphasized the enormous importance of friendship: of having younger friends and making new ones, because the sad fact is our old friends keep on dying.

However, Karen advises, always be sure to take the time to "cherish and nurture your long-standing friendships as a living link between the present and past." These are the friends, she urges us to remember, who "loved you when—and who love you now."

On a more practical note, Richard writes that since we're—all of us—"a mix of good and bad," we should seek out those whose good outweighs the bad, rather than engaging in what would surely be a fruitless search for perfection. "There may be angels among us," he wryly observes, "but I am not sure how many I have run into."

There is also a lot of advice about the importance of continued learning and growing, with an emphasis on the need to challenge ourself, move out of our comfort zone, and get better at adapting to altered circumstances. Gordon urges us to "be creative, do something new," whether it's "knit or bake . . . or tutor an immigrant." Margaret tells us don't be afraid of change. And Barb points out that no matter how firm our plans for the future may be, "LIFE WILL INTERVENE," and we will find ourself being challenged, like it or not. And so her advice is "BE FLEXIBLE," which isn't all that easy in our fifth-fifth, but can help us escape the rigidity which, Barb warns, is likely to "rob life of its many joys."

Betty strongly advises us to not depend on our children for our social life.

"Have your own circle of friends. Build a life for yourself around your own interests and expectations. . . . When they [your children] see you being active and involved," she reassures us, "they will want to see more of you."

She also warns us to "never offer advice or even a helpful suggestion to your daughter-in-law," though mothers, she hastens to add, can always advise their own children—it's their job.

Kindness and integrity are the focus of Mary's response to my wisdom query.

"I have not always been kind, and I have not always brought integrity to my actions," she writes. "But I hope that there is a trend upward. . . ." Elaborating on the value of kindness, she adds, "I find that when I offer an act of kindness to another, there is a moment, a space created, when both of us—the one offering and the one receiving—experience something. Call it grace, call it connection with one's humanity—it feels good. And, just for that moment, it leaves the world a better place."

Monica, who has found at the age of eighty the capacity to live in the here and now, has this to say about her journey to get there: "As a young woman, as a girl even, I lived in the future, dreaming of college and a handsome husband and children. When the children came and grew, I found myself living in the past, remembering when they were born . . . took their first steps . . . went off to school. I am old now and living in the present, much more peaceful than I've ever been."

Monica says she is well aware of the unpredictability of what lies ahead, including its potential for sorrow and suffering. She is also aware, with some regret, "that I never appreciated the present as much as I should." So having made whatever practical plans can be made for the future, "I am, perhaps for the first time in my life, living life to the fullest—right now."

For ninety-year-old Tersh the answer to my wisdom query was unequivocal: wisdom, to him, is the acceptance of death. And when we arranged to meet so we could talk a little more about his response, he assured me that though he loves our RC, and loves the many people he has met here, and even loves the food—particularly the soups and the desserts—he is not afraid of death and is ready to die. He's got all his papers in order—the will, the POA, the DNR, the whatevers—though he hasn't yet decided where, exactly, he'd like his ashes to be strewn. Age "gradually closes windows of opportunity," he explains, which helps prepare us to prepare for death.

Tersh says that an acceptance of death is going to make life easier not just for those of us who are soon to die, but also for our family and our friends. However, he adds—and this is a big however—just because he's *ready* to die doesn't mean he's in any rush to do so.

"Being here," he tells me, "is a great joy. I wouldn't mind living another four or five years."

In contrast to Tersh's heartfelt response are these three brisk and witty wisdom one-liners:

From Penny on choosing a partner: "Dependable is better than unpredictable—unless you'd rather be terrified than bored."

From George on using email: "Think twice before you push the 'send' button."

From Roz on winning arguments: "If you always have to be right, you're going to be a very lonely person."

Jinks charmingly provides this important reminder of the limits of our control: "The good news?—you are in the passenger seat. The bad news?—you are in the *passenger* seat. Remember that while you've got all the responsibility for your life, you are not in control—you are not driving the bus."

Bob, in a carefully nuanced reply, makes this distinction between "important" and "urgent": In my work and personal life there were times when "what was merely urgent tended to crowd out the truly important." Having the good judgment to know which is which—"both short- and long-term, and acting accordingly"—is "a critical aspect of wisdom (and how to live)."

I'm adding these words *about* wisdom from Leonard, my late and dearly beloved rabbi friend: "It is human to be ignorant and to achieve wisdom slowly and painfully, to be humbled by our experience . . . to be confused and bewildered by the turmoil and complexity of life."

There were many other thoughtful and heartfelt and often extensive replies to my wisdom query, urging that we be true to ourself, emphasizing (especially for men) the value of taking the time to build relationships, questioning what's more important, wisdom or luck, and encouraging us to keep moving and to stay active both intellectually and physically. All of these are valuable, but I want to especially highlight the words of the lively, interesting, smart, and utterly delightful-to-be-with Bunty, a hundred-year-old woman who still makes beautiful quilts and glass artworks, is still an enthusiast of bridge and chess, and understands the power of poetry:

For me the one important ingredient of my abundant life is that I have a mantra that I unconsciously look at or say to myself every day. . . .

I am a part of all that I have met;
Yet all experience is an arch wherethro'
Gleams that untravell'd world whose margin fades
For ever and for ever when I move.

Thank you, Alfred, Lord Tennyson and your inspiration, "Ulysses."

Like Bunty, I love "Ulysses," because it encourages old folks like us to pass through that arch and into the untraveled world—wherever, for each of us, that arch is located, and whatever, for each of us, that world might be. Because, despite our age, there are among us those who wish "to strive, to seek, to find, and not to yield." Because, "though much is taken, much abides." Because "death closes all but . . . ere the end, some work of noble note may yet be done."

Well, maybe we're deluding ourself but these encouraging words can help to get us out of bed every morning.

And when I need even more assistance to get myself up and out and into my life, I turn to poet Jack Gilbert's powerful prayer:

> Teach me mortality.
> Frighten me into the present.
> Help me to find the heft of these days.

And for really dark days I have memorized Adam Zagajewski's "Try to Praise the Mutilated World," which I first read a few days after 9/11, and which promises that, despite its disappearance, we will someday see the return of "the gentle light."

If you're looking for more words of wisdom, read some poetry. If you want to possess those words, memorize poems. They will educate, illuminate, inspire, and console you. Maybe they will even make you wise.

*

Now, I intend no disrespect when I say it's important to keep in mind that conveying words of wisdom isn't quite the same as actually being wise. Most of us, I suspect, are better at talking the talk than we are at walking the walk. Most of us, I suspect— and I very much include myself—tend to sound wiser than we actually live.

As for definitions of "wisdom" and "wise," I've encountered plenty of them, though warned by one scholarly paper that "we have yet to reach a scientific consensus." So I've chosen, from a feast of definitions and descriptions, those qualities of wisdom I found spoke most compellingly to me:

Wisdom requires some basic knowledge gained through education, and perspective and judgment gained through life experience. It draws on intuition as well as logic; it draws on emotion as well as the intellect; it includes curiosity, flexibility, practicality, and perseverance. And it isn't afraid of not knowing or new ideas.

Being wise would also involve significant *self*-knowledge— of our strengths and vulnerabilities, of our limits and possibilities, of what we can and cannot and should not do. This self-understanding should be combined with an understanding of others, and an interest in and empathic concern for friends and family and lovers that allow us to sustain enduring relationships.

I also want to select from the definitions of "wisdom" and

"wise" a grasp of life's complexities, contradictions, absurdities, moral ambiguities. And I want to include some kind of spiritual growth, some kind of evolving self-transcendence, that eventually allows us to experience our individual life within the larger context of LIFE in all its mystery, difficulty, and grandeur.

Finally, though I can't remember having seen it mentioned much among all the definitions I encountered, I want "wisdom" and "wise" to include a sense of humor, for I find it hard to imagine trying to deal with life's absurdities without one.

I'm sure that I have left out some crucial qualities of wisdom and being wise. I'm sure I'll hear about them.

Although, like Richard, who hasn't run into many angels among us, it's unlikely that we've met many (or any) whose wisdom encompasses all of the above. It's also unlikely that we, overachievers though we may be, would comfortably count ourselves among the wise. At best, we're wise on some days and wise in some ways; wise about some things, not so wise about others. And certainly wise enough to know that there's plenty that we don't know—and never will.

Last week my older granddaughter, in regard to some horrific newspaper headline, sent me an email asking, "Do you have something wise and comforting you could say about this?" To which, feeling deeply inadequate, I reluctantly, regretfully answered, "No."

Because sometimes the only possible answer is no. But sometimes—using our brain and our heart and a little help from our friends—we can stumble and fumble our way into a "yes."

Because, as I've been stating, restating, and hoping and praying it's true, we're not done yet. We're old, but we've learned a few things. We could learn a few more. We're old, but there's too much going on to ignore. We're old, but there's still time before it's all over.

And because we're old, we've got this—we're told—"slight advantage" that may make us wiser than we used to be. So we need to get down on our creaky old knees and start planting, because now is the next-best time to plant a tree.

Prescription

for Dr. Collin Cullen

Reupholster, or not reupholster—that is the question.
It is hard for us in our nineties to plan ahead.
Two of my living room chairs have gotten quite threadbare.
But wait! Will the new fabric get here before I am dead?

At our age—or so that old joke goes—don't buy green
    bananas.
A two-year subscription? Read a short story instead.
My chairs, if reupholstered, would look so much better.
But I might not know how they're looking because I'd be dead.

So I talked with my doctor after my annual checkup.
All of the tests had been given, the lab reports read.
Planning is hard, I complained, for us in our nineties.
You just never know where when why how or if you'll be dead.

He wrote a prescription for me.
Reupholster, it said.

Epilogue

In March 2020 Covid came to our RC, as it did to institutions all over the world. But thanks to the precautions and restrictions installed by the management, it didn't run rampant here. We're done now with the masking, the social distancing, the limitations on visiting, the individual dinners in bags delivered nightly to our apartment door. And when cases of Covid crop up, as they still on occasion do, we who contract the virus dutifully take Paxlovid and follow the quarantine rules.

At the end of 2022, Milton went to the hospital for what, to our surprise, turned out to be Covid, but was symptom free within a couple of days. The doctors said I could take him home the next morning. Instead, with me sleeping soundly in the reclining chair beside his hospital bed, he quietly died in the middle of the night.

I hadn't said goodbye because he wasn't supposed to die—he was coming home.

Some months after Milton's death I heard a rabbi give a sermon in the course of which she spoke of four things that we might consider saying at the bedside of a dying beloved: Forgive me. I forgive you. Thank you. I love you.

I felt she had read my heart—so full of sorrow for not saying goodbye to Milton. I felt that she was speaking directly to me.

Forgive me. I forgive you. Milton and I, two scrappy, strong-willed people, often had good reason to say these words, or at least some version of these words. And we both were very generous, very comfortably free and easy with our I-love-yous. And it's not that I didn't say thank you when Milton did something that courteous people say thank you for. But since his death I'd been haunted with overpowering regret for failing to say something much larger than that: a formal, global, embracing, almost ceremonial THANK YOU for all that he had given me over the decades that we had been husband and wife.

In the Jewish tradition, a year or so after someone has died, there is a graveside service known as an unveiling, where the covering of the stone marking the grave is removed, and prayers are said and some reminiscences offered. I decided that, after each of my children and grandchildren spoke a few words at Milton's unveiling, I'd take this opportunity to finally say my formal thank-you to him.

And so I did. And here is what I said:

Thank you for being you—a loving, decent, interesting, smart, and sexy man.

Thank you for being such a devoted dad to our three sons, helping them to become the beautiful men that they've become, and reveling in fatherhood and grandfatherhood and everyday family life as if they were the most precious gifts on earth.

Thank you for being—long before the Women's Movement told you to be—an equal partner in the tasks of our household, sharing our many domestic and childcare duties with great competence and goodwill. Without your doing all this as well as always encouraging me and cheering me on, I, who hadn't had one word in print till after we were married, would never have had the breathing space or the time to realize my dream of becoming a published writer.

And finally I want to thank you for having the boldness, the sheer audacity, to have given me—to have given our whole family—a larger and far more exciting life than I'd have been daring enough to create on my own.

A life of joy, adventure, productivity, and social responsibility. A life of intense, entangled, enduring love.

A Few Endnotes

EPIGRAPH

In the meantime . . . enjoy not being dead. This excellent suggestion, to which I added the word "In," is an edited version of "Not to say the meantime isn't as good a time as any to enjoy not being dead," from the poem "The Magic Rule of Nine," by Joan Retallack.

OLD

All the quotes from Angell in this book come from his essay "This Old Man," the *New Yorker*, February 17 and 24, 2014.

LOSING IT

The Andrews sisters—Patty, Maxene, and LaVerne—were among the most popular singing groups of the 1940s.

WHAT'S LEFT

If the story of Peg sounds familiar, it's because I've told it before with a different name and slightly different details. I kept loosely in touch with her until she finally left Washington, still quite bewildered by her social abandonment.

Making meaning: I chose this term because I believe we're mainly on our own in our last phase of life and need to create our own personal reason for being.

COUNTING THE DEAD

This essay originally appeared in *Moment* magazine, January/February 2021.

Miltown: A widely prescribed tranquilizer, launched in the 1950s. Known to some as the "happy pill."

Daisy Mae: The spectacularly curvaceous young woman hopelessly in love with the cartoon character Li'l Abner in the comic strip of the same name, which ran in newspapers from 1934 to 1977.

Nancy Drew: Smart and good-looking and practically perfect, Nancy was the mystery-solving young heroine of the Nancy Drew mystery series, a vast number of books launched in 1930 and written under the pseudonym Carolyn Keene.

WHAT ELSE I REMEMBER

Below is a little more information about several cultural references from way back when, though if you're my age you're probably familiar with most of them.

Liz Taylor's Seven Husbands: Conrad Hilton Jr., Michael Wilding, Mike Todd, Eddie Fisher, Richard Burton, John Warner, Larry Fortensky. (Though married *eight* times she only had seven husbands because she married Richard Burton twice.)

Snow White's Seven Dwarfs: Dopey, Happy, Sneezy, Sleepy, Grumpy, Bashful, Doc.

"Mairzy Doats": A mystifyingly popular song whose lyrics sound nonsensical until they're sung slowly and carefully enunciated; thus "Mairzy doats and dozy doats" becomes "Mares eat oats and does eat oats," etc. After which they still sound pretty nonsensical.

Brylcreem: A hair cream for men, advertised by a singing commercial that starts, "Brylcreem—a little dab'll do ya . . ."

J-E-L-L-O: A singing commercial for you-know-what.

Hubba-hubba: An expression of excitement or approval, particularly over a person's appearance.

Jack, Doc, and Reggie: The heroes of a radio program called *I Love a Mystery*, about three friends who run a detective agency which boasts "no job too tough, no adventure too baffling."

The Edsel: A famous failure of a car, described as "overhyped, unattractive, and low quality."

Betty Boop: a baby-faced, big-eyed, animated cartoon character, something of a caricatured Jazz Age flapper, featured in 1930s movies.

AFTERWARD

The three poems in the body of this essay and a fourth poem following it were published previously as follows: "My Legacy," from *Nearing Ninety*, Viorst; "On Not Being a Good Sport About the Fact That I'm Going to Die One of These Days," from *I'm Too Young to*

Be Seventy, Viorst; Mortal Question," from *Suddenly Sixty*, Viorst; "An Afterlife," from *Unexpectedly Eighty*, Viorst.

For further information on terror management, check out the work of social psychologist Sheldon Solomon and his colleagues.

HAPPINESS

See Diana Athill's *Alive, Alive Oh!*, pages 2, 5–6, for the quoted material, and read the whole book for her refreshing observations on old age.

Scientific studies about a Gratitude Journal, and the mental and physical benefits of gratitude, are referenced in the *New York Times*, June 10, 2023, A3.

We next reach the heights of happiness in old age. Recent studies show a dramatic decline in the happiness of American youth under thirty. But although our young now have a happiness ranking of merely sixty-two out of the hundred and forty-three countries surveyed, those over sixty are ranked at a happy ten, which means that while the Happiness Curve may show fewer years of happiness for the young, its direction still remains onward and upward after an earlier, longer midlife malaise. From "U.S. Happiness Score Drops Amid a Youth 'Midlife Crisis,' " *Washington Post*, March 21, 2024, A2.

LONELINESS

See Dr. Vivek Murthy's "Our Epidemic of Loneliness and Isolation: The U.S. Surgeon General's Advisory on the Healing Effects of Social Connection and Community," U.S. Public Health Service, 2023.

So what's to be done about helping lonely folks? For an interesting discussion of this question, see Nicholas Kristof, "We Know the Cure for Loneliness. So Why Do We Suffer?" *New York Times*, September 7, 2023, A27. See also Eleanor Cummins and Andrew Zaleski, "If Loneliness Is an Epidemic, How Do We Treat It?" *New York Times*, July 16, 2023, 6–7.

COMMUNITY

"living, breathing human beings." See Kristof reference above.

WISDOM

The quote "certain life experiences tend to be wisdom producing" comes from Ivan Oosthuizen, "Are Older People Wiser?," Center for Practical Wisdom, University of Chicago, May 4, 2021.

Other replies to my wisdom query:

> "Don't tie yourself into a pretzel and be untrue to who you are in order to be hired, admired, or loved."—Liz

> "Especially for men. Slow down. Build relationships. One day you'll be glad you did."—Neal

"As someone who has been more lucky than wise in my own life, I sometimes wonder whether it isn't more important to be lucky than wise—notwithstanding the truth that one's luck is partly or maybe largely what one makes of it. But one never knows, do one? (Fats Waller's wisdom)."—Bob

"Keep moving!"—Dorothy (a dancer still dancing at the age of eighty-nine)

"My advice is to stay physically and intellectually active . . . in all aspects of your life. . . . Nurture a curiosity about anything and everything. Why is the sky blue? Can I fix this broken table? What happened on this date? What is the background of someone you just met? . . . Learn about flowers, trees, and birds."—Ted

The lines starting "Teach me mortality . . ." are from Jack Gilbert's poem "I Imagine the Gods," in *The Great Fires: Poems 1982–1992*.

"we have yet to reach a scientific consensus" is from Ivan Oosthuizen, "Are Older People Wiser?"

AND FINALLY

Most of the interviews for this book were conducted between early 2023 and late 2024.

Acknowledgments

Many, many women and men most generously and eloquently talked to me about life in their Final Fifth, the term I've used to designate (give or take a few birthdays) those years between ages eighty and a hundred. Some, like me, are living in a retirement community. Some are not. Most allowed me to use their first names and their undisguised life stories. Some did not. But even when I've been asked, or chose, to change people's names or blur a few details, the essence of their stories remains intact. I thank them for those stories. I thank them all.

I don't think I have the space it would take to thank all my friends—old and young—who encouraged me in the writing of this book. You know who you are, and you surely know how very grateful I am for your support. I do, however, want to mention my agent and friend, Susan Ramer, and my excellent new editor Mindy Marques, for receiving this book from the start with open arms, as well as Johanna Li, who meticulously watched over its every phase. And I must express particular thanks to Li Schorr and Michael Joseph and Ruth Anne Keister, who in countless ways graciously and patiently made my life easier.

And finally, because their loving presence in my life has made it so much sweeter to grow old, I want to thank my sons—Tony and Nick and Alexander; and my daughters-in-law—Michelle and Marya and Marla; and my grandchildren—Miranda, Bryce, Nathaniel, Benjamin, Olivia, Isaac, and Toby; and my almost-daughter, Jeannette, her husband Steve, and their son Daniel.

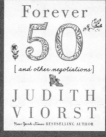
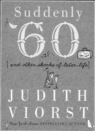

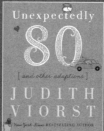
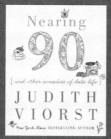